About the Author:

BERNARD BASSET, S.J., one of the most popular and appealing spiritual writers of our time, is the author of such other best-selling Image Books as *How to Be Really with It*, *The Noonday Devil*, *We Agnostics*, *We Neurotics*, and *Let's Start Praying Again*. Well known for his retreats as well, he travels extensively in the United States each year, and is currently a parish priest on the Isles of Scilly in Cornwall, England. Here he offers what he calls "a breezy book on a somber subject, the confession and forgiveness of sin. Any such book must be cheerful," he goes on, "for few happier experiences than forgiveness are known to man." A writer of extraordinary wit and sensitivity, Father Basset possesses a rare talent for both uplifting and sustaining the reader—physically as well as spiritually. His encouraging words of wisdom have inspired hope and strength in tens of thousands of Christians who have struggled with their faith.

About the Book:

"[Father Basset] writes easily and with an eye to modernity, with references to psychiatry, guilt, tensions and other aspects of the current scene. He puts the matter of confession into historical perspective, giving us copious quotes from sources as diverse as St. Teresa of Ávila, Sigmund Freud, William James, Cardinal Newman, among others. . . . [This] informative and timely reflection on [confession] is presented in the relaxed, warmhearted style that Basset has accustomed us to expect of him. As such, it makes a definite contribution to the subject and contains material of interest both to those who favor the confessional and those who have doubts about it."

(America)

GUILTY, O LORD

Guilty, O Lord

Yes, I still go to confession

BERNARD BASSET, S.J.

IMAGE BOOKS

A Division of Doubleday & Company, Inc.
Garden City, New York
1976

Image Books edition by special arrangement with Doubleday & Company, Inc.
Image Books edition published February 1976

This book was originally published in England by Sheed and Ward, Ltd. under the title *Guilty, My Lord*

Nihil obstat: F. J. Bartlett, Censor. *Imprimatur:* David Norris, Vicar General Westminster, October 15, 1973

Library of Congress Cataloging in Publication Data

Basset, Bernard.
   Guilty, O Lord; yes, I still go to confession.

   British ed. published under title: Guilty, my Lord.
   1. Confession.   I.   Title.
BX2265.2.B323   1975   234'.166
ISBN: 0-385-11372-2

To the memory
of my dear brother
Fr. Edmund Basset, S.J.
who died in May

CONTENTS

1—GUILTY, O LORD

Here is a breezy book on a somber subject, the confession and forgiveness of sin. Any such book must be cheerful for few happier experiences than forgiveness are known to man. With what relief we owned up in childhood, no matter how angry our loving parents pretended to be. After a tissue of lies and false pretenses, it was a joy to be both wicked and free. One of St. Thomas More's daughters admitted later that she used to be deliberately naughty for the very pleasure of being forgiven by him.

The child is father of the man. As we grow older confession and forgiveness may not be so simple but they are twice as sweet. In the case of lovers, nothing promotes the match better than the tearful reconciliation after a trivial tiff. Every happy marriage is a mosaic of mistakes, sorrow and forgiveness, every understanding friendship implies just this. Dorothy Sayers put this well. "Forgiveness is not a doing-away with consequences; nor is it, primarily, a remission of punishment. A child may be forgiven and 'let off' punishment or punished and then forgiven, either way may bring good results. But no good will come of leaving him unpunished and unforgiven. Forgiveness is the reestablishment of a right relationship in which the parties can genuinely feel and behave as freely with one another as though the unhappy incident had never taken place."[1]

If confession and forgiveness are essential in human relations, they are of infinite importance in man's rela-

tionship with God. Wherever man has existed, sin has
flourished and sin leads to sorrow and that yearning for
forgiveness, so central a theme in the New Testament
and in the Old. The subject is far wider than the Bible
for if, in length, it takes us back to Adam, in width it
embraces all the four corners of the earth. I have been
reading about the potential liturgies in ancient Greece,
India, Tibet, Peru. One of the problems in a book on
such a subject must be the vastness of the area to be
covered and its complexity.

Happily, my book has a practical purpose which
need not involve us in the penitential rites of ancient
Peru.[2] The need for confession and forgiveness is basic
to human nature and we may examine this in the con-
text of the Christian faith. Though we thus reduce the
subject, it still remains vast.

In Christian literature there are books upon books
dealing with sin, sorrow, and forgiveness from a legal
point of view. These tell us about mortal and venial
sin, lay down the laws governing confession and the
formulas to be used. On other shelves in the library,
the theology of sin and forgiveness is treated, involving
us in the whole story of the incarnation down to
Christ's death on the cross. Then there are the apolo-
getic books in which the practice of confession is
defended in a hostile world. On these shelves we might
find the works of Luther, Calvin, Zwingli, St. John
Fisher and St. Thomas More. Nor should we ignore
the pious books about confession, sometimes irrever-
ently called "the tear-jerkers," sermons by great
revivalists with John Bunyan in the van. Some of these
aspects of sin and forgiveness may be touched on later
but none are essential to my theme. It is the psychology of sin and forgiveness which most concerns me at
the moment and this is an approach not often treated
in books.

The sacrament of penance is under great pressure at the moment, in a changing world. Conflicting theories, criticisms, practices are causing much confusion and not a little misery. There are those who loved the old dispensation and resent all changes and those whose faith in the sacrament is fast fading away. I am a middle-of-the-roader, happy but mildly apprehensive; too many babies have been thrown out with the bath water in these progressive days.

In a period of drift and confusion, it has seemed to me important to re-examine both sides of the question and then to make up my mind for myself. One must sift the essentials from the nonessentials, accept changes but, even in pontifical circles, count one's change.

Though my views about confession have expanded and deepened, I look back to the practices of childhood days with affection, not regret. Along with many of you, I took confession for granted from my tenderest years. I made my first confession at the age of six in Westminster Cathedral, fifty-eight years ago. They told me only after it was over that the ancient Monsignor who absolved me was stone deaf.

As child, schoolboy, student I liked confessing my sins. It cost nothing and gave me the kind of gesture of sorrow that I wanted to make. Later in life, I would witness the "children's confessions" in large city parishes, during which the Church would be transformed into a battlefield or marketplace. Hitler, who confessed as a child in similar conditions, once described the pandemonium. No pressure was exerted in my schooldays to get us into the box.

The situation altered slightly after I became a priest. Priests, also, need forgiveness and must practice what they preach. In many ways, confession is more irksome for a priest. For him, it often means a special journey to dig out a colleague who knows him well. If his sins are small he feels foolish thus to disturb his neighbor, if large, he feels ashamed of himself. Happily, among priests, confession is a routine business with an unemotional approach. Looking back, I chuckle at an incident in Boston some eighteen years ago. Having just arrived from Britain, I tracked down an ancient Jesuit to his room. Boston was roasting in a heat wave; I found my confessor relaxing in his rocking chair and reading the psalms of David in the nude. I turned towards the door, embarrassed, but he said blandly, "Confession, Father: be kind enough to pass me my stole."

It just so happens that I am writing about confession at a moment in life when I cannot get to confession easily. Living as I do on the Isles of Scilly, out in the East Atlantic, the sacrament would cost me a flight by helicopter to Penzance. No sin that I commit on these simple islands is worth £7.

Over my years as a priest, the reality of sin and the joy of receiving absolution has been brought home to me in three different ways. The experience which opens one's eyes to the psychology of forgiveness is the assisting of a patient who is going to die. In such situations, the personality of the priest counts for very little, it is forgiveness that the dying man yearns for and which brings with it an overwhelming relief. I saw with my own two eyes both sorrow and happiness visible on a human face. On more routine occasions, the sacrament may sometimes appear banal and boring; in the final crisis one experiences the bond between happiness and faith.

Were I to pretend that my life had been spent ministering to the dying, I would have to catch the next helicopter to Penzance. Certainly the experience of hearing a last confession is deeply rewarding to any priest. For me there has been a second revelation of the power of forgiveness during the thirty years in which I have directed retreats. A retreat is more than a series of talks or a casual conference: it is a valid form of spiritual therapy. During retreats, the director spends the best part of the day listening to the problems and worries of many people, some of whom are facing agonizing situations with courage which he cannot claim himself.

This second experience of the power of forgiveness differs slightly from that known when attending a patient at death. While listening to the troubles of the living, one comes across the ravages caused by a sense of guilt. Oddly enough, the dying move into a sphere which is out of reach of guilt. Just as a patient in hospital achieves peace by surrendering to the doctors, so the dying man recovers his equilibrium when he commits himself entirely, with all his sins, to God. No firm purpose of amendment is required at the time of death. Those suffer guilt who must go home and reach decisions not required by the pilgrim at the journey's end.

I must have directed retreats for tens of thousands over these thirty years. Such statistics do not prove me holy, only that I know a thing or two. Nor are retreatants all retired ladies or maidens crossed in love. Almost my first retreat was given in wartime Britain to seventy Royal Air Force personnel. My last, three months ago, was to sixty assorted farmers in Pineville, Louisiana. To this retreat one client brought his tape recorder but not to flatter me. A poultry farmer with sixty thousand hens, he could not face two nights without them; a tape played quietly in the early morning saved him from melancholy.

The third experience which so greatly helped and

surprised me has been the desperate need of so many to get things off their chest. The satisfaction of owning up, which so many of us knew in childhood, quickly becomes a habit and persists. Doctors, lawyers, nurses, priests, even policemen are well aware of this.

Such an experience as this contradicts the popular impression that men and women dislike confessing their sins. They may find the ritual irksome or the confessional box offputting but the desire to tell someone of their behavior proves a built-in safety valve. I have seen this in hospital with patients—of no religion and total strangers—who will grab an opportunity to speak about their sins. One saw the same with soldiers in wartime and among civilians huddled in air raid shelters in the blitz. With Alcoholics Anonymous such public confession is rightly regarded as a therapy. Moral rearmament groups delighted to testify to past misdemeanors while, at a Pentecostal meeting recently, I listened to a young priest in Boston urged, apparently by the Spirit, to stand up and spout about his sins. Though such a performance seemed to me slightly artificial, I stuffed my handkerchief into my mouth to discourage the Holy Ghost.

It is not just the godly who like speaking about their sins for the ungodly are still more voluble. This may be seen at any bar among those who have had one too much. Alcohol makes many a man maudlin and he then weeps over his past wickedness. As one funny man said to me, "If you want us to make a good confession, why not place a bottle of Scotch at the head of the queue?"

Fooling apart, how much it helps us to share our guilt. I have met those who dislike confessing to a priest, who dislike the confessional, but it is rare indeed to meet someone who dislikes talking about past sins. How many, in our day, to gain such an opportunity, gladly pay a psychiatrist.

At this point allow me to introduce Dr. Paul Tournier, the distinguished Swiss psychiatrist. Dr. Tournier is a devout Calvinist. He writes with deep understanding of the value of confessing our sins. In the first passage that I quote, he is answering the charge of some theologians that he is playing the part of the priest. He replies:

I have often written about confession already but the misunderstanding still persists. The fear has been expressed by theologians that I am enlisting the doctor to take the place of the priest. I have not done so and never shall. That the Roman Catholic must seek sacramental absolution, that we must urge him to do so and that he cannot excuse himself on the pretext that he has confessed to his doctor—all this is clear: one cannot make one's peace with God by cheating one's church.

But the theologians must see things as they really are and not as they would like them to be. There are around us vast numbers of people who are sick for confession, even among Roman Catholics and Eastern Christians, even among those who go regularly and sincerely to confession and who may suddenly, in a personal conversation, realise that they are guilty of wrongs that are of much more decisive importance for their lives than any they have so far confessed. Moreover there are those who have kept away from their church precisely to escape confession and who will be able to return to it as a result of a liberating hour spent with their doctor.

And, then, there are the Protestants, among whom the practice of confession has fallen into grave disuse. Pastor Thurian has recently recalled with what clear insistence the reformers enjoined the regular practice of confession. Lastly there are the unbelievers, the half-

believers, the agnostics and even those who are violently
and aggressively anti-religious. They have as much need
as believers of expressing their remorse.[3]

Here Dr. Tournier makes many a capital point. We do
not go to confession because the Church tells us but
because we need to for our fulfillment and happiness. I
like his sentence "There are around us vast numbers of
people who are sick for confession" for this exactly
meets my own experience. Lack of confession may in
time induce a deep spiritual sickness, the symptoms of
which are widespread today. A devout Christian psychiatrist and a retreat director are both aware of this.

The old adage *Mens sana in corpore sano* contains
more than a grain of truth. If a sound mind depends
on a healthy body, so does a healthy body require a
sound mind. The medical men of today, more fully accepting the power of mind over matter, publish lists of
physical illnesses mentally induced. If we take just one
further step backwards, it is easy to see the power of
the spiritual over body and mind alike. A sick soul
plays havoc with our mental balance and may cause ul-
cers and indigestion, too. A deep and enduring sense of
guilt corrodes the toughest life. I have noticed over
thirty years a rapid increase in tension and much of
this in origin is spiritual. In the headlong flight from
fear, loneliness, and failure, men fall back on drink and
drugs or forward into deep depression and, with Hamlet, think about suicide. In a recent study of suicide,
the estimate was given for countries who keep accurate
records of a thousand suicides a day. Such figures cannot include the number of fatal accidents permitted by
those who have no wish to live.

In the gospel story, the recurring link between sin
and sickness is greatly emphasized. I grow more and

more certain that such a connection is valid and should not be brushed aside.

Four hundred years ago, in Tudor London, Sir Thomas More, the man for all seasons, made this very point. He was competing with his children in their homework and, it would seem, dashed off an English essay on *The Four Last Things*. In his quaint and endearing English, he pointed out to his children the ravages caused by certain sins on the human face:

> Now let us see what help we may have of this medicine against the sickness of envy which is, undoubtedly, both a sore torment and a very consumption. For surely, envy is such a torment as all the tyrants in Sicily never devised a sorer. And it so drinks up the moisture of the body and consumes the good blood, so discolours the face, so defaces the beauty, so disfigures the visage, leaving it all bony, lean, pale and wan, that a person, well set-a-work with envy, needs no other image of death than his own face in a glass.[4]

The bottling up of such a spiritual sickness as envy may lead to nervous breakdowns and to melancholy. Four hundred years after Thomas More, Dr. Tournier, drawing on his clinical experience, makes the same point. He writes:

> I could give very many examples especially of patients who have come to visit me only once—often from a great distance—with the sole purpose of finding someone to whom they can confess a sin that has been weighing them down for years. They are often bewildering cases in which I have done nothing, practically said nothing for which I have done no more than silently pray. Or, perhaps, I have by a few kind words helped them to make their confession more concrete. There remains nothing for me to do but remind them, in one way or another, that "If we confess our sins, he is faith-

ful and righteous to forgive our sins and to cleanse us
from all unrighteousness" (1 John 1:9). In many cases I
have had neither time nor opportunity to make a medical examination or to prescribe a medicine and yet, a little while later, I have received a letter telling me that
some morbid symptom that no medical treatment had
been able to cure has disappeared, either at once or
gradually.[3]

If Dr. Tournier is right, and my long experience as
both a sinner and a confessor supports him, confession
is a crying need today. How accurate his diagnosis that
thousands around us are sick for confession and how
sure his assertion that many tensions and morbid
symptoms derive from this deficiency. Tournier is not
alone among psychiatrists in this. William James
writes feelingly about the value of confession, as does
Dr. Viktor Frankl in his *The Doctor and the Soul.*
How strange that while the psychiatrists stress the ther-
apeutic value of confession and forgiveness, Christians,
reared in the tradition of the sacrament, are dis-
satisfied.

The sacrament of penance is now out of favor, and a
practice which we in childhood took very much for
granted is now disregarded or spoken of with scorn. Far
be it from me to condemn such Christians and their
dissatisfaction for this in itself seems to point to something wrong. In recent years, in every retreat, at every
question-and-answer session, queries about confession
have pride of place. Let this be the justification for my
book.

I find no case of a sinner in the gospel who
approached Christ for forgiveness and went away sad.
The Samaritan woman, with a tally of seven men, left
Christ so excited that she had to tell the whole village
of her relief. That shrewd little taxgatherer, Zacheus,

whipped out his checkbook just as soon as he could scramble down from that sycamore tree. It was his suggestion that he should pay fourfold for past deceits. Christ paid no attention when Peter said, "Depart from me for I am a sinful man, O Lord."

2—OUT OF THE DEPTHS

To appreciate the malice of sin and the joy of forgiveness, we need first to know ourselves. We are not flat fish. We have depths and three dimensions and live on three levels simultaneously. As the great Austrian psychiatrist Dr. Viktor Frankl puts it, "Man lives in three dimensions, the somatic, the mental, and the spiritual."[1] Just as a motorist takes his automatic gears for granted, so we move from one dimension to another without conscious thought. It pays, however, to know something of these three dimensions if we are to understand ourselves.

When I was young, man was presumed to have only two dimensions, and every good Christian child, well instructed, knew that man was made up of body and soul. Such a division is now outdated but by no means false. Just as gallons and pints will long survive the introduction of the metric system, so John Brown's body will lie a-moldering in the grave while his soul goes marching on.

The division of man into body and soul is useful but restrictive; it fails to tell the full story, it tends to provide an inaccurate picture of an unreal world. We come to regard our bodies as lumpish, lazy, and mulish and our souls as bright, ethereal, ghostly, something of will-o'-the-wisp. Nearly everyone presumes that the soul lives inside the body, when things may well be the other way round. After all, my memory may jump back fifty years in a second, while my body remains seated and gulping down a can of Diet Coke. Many a time, my heart communes with friends across the Atlantic without trying to take my body along. When his sister St. Scholastica died, St. Benedict saw her soul winging away towards heaven as a dove: while not for a moment doubting the great saint's vision, we might think that he was seeing a thing or two.

Advances in two very different fields of learning throw doubt on the competence of the body-soul approach. Scripture scholars point out that such a view was unknown in the early part of the Bible and that the great patriarchs saw man as a whole. The division of man into body and soul was Greek in origin and, with the rapid spread of Greek culture, worked its way into later Hebrew thought. But when Christ cried on the cross, "Father, into Thy hands I commend my spirit," may we say that he meant by spirit exactly what we mean by soul?

If modern Scripture scholars deserve our attention, so do modern psychologists. At the turn of the century psychology, as we now know it, was in its early infancy. Through half a century of astonishing growth, psychology has taught us to think of man as an individual person, with body and soul fusing to produce a whole. The apple tree in my garden achieves just this when roots, trunk, leaves, and sap work together, play their parts, and survive in the new fruit.

This theory which sounds so novel is, in fact, as old as the hills. Poets, philosophers, mystics, without using psychological jargon, have known about the three dimensions for centuries. As I hope to show later—this is a vital point in any approach to confession—Christ emphasized the three dimensions consistently. As for the rest, each poet, mystic, thinker has his or her individual way of describing our composition but the three dimensions of human consciousness stay the same. Dr.

Frankl states categorically, "Man lives in three dimensions, the somatic, the mental, and the spiritual," to which an audience of experts, headed by St. Teresa of Ávila and St. Augustine, would certainly reply, "Hear! Hear!"

St. Teresa of Avila is forever writing of the higher and lower parts of the soul. She is, also, an expert at mixing metaphors and has no sooner asked us to "turn to our castle with its many mansions" when she breaks off to exclaim, "Think of the palmito."[2] The point of the palmito, as she explains, is that it has many layers of outer rind which need removing before the savory center is exposed. St. Augustine discovered two wills in himself and after many years of effort came to identify the higher or deeper one with his heart.

From different viewpoints, the experts saw the three dimensions in different ways. For William James, there were the "Once Born" and the "Twice Born" and, in the center of our being, the "Red Hot Point" of consciousness. Freud recognized the Super-Ego, the Ego, and the Id. Dr. Sherwood Taylor preferred simple headings, our public life, our private life, and our inner life. In his *I'm OK—You're OK* Dr. Thomas Harris is highly original; each baby is born with a built-in tape recorder and three tapes, recording simultaneously.[3] Our *Parental* tape records the rules laid down by parents, priests, and teachers; the *Baby* tape gives our childish reactions; the *Adult* tape, by a process of selection, puts together our personal and mature point of view. For good measure, let me end this paragraph with Shakespeare, whose genius could present the three dimensions on the stage. So we see Hamlet, the young and popular prince of Denmark, talking to himself in secret, and choosing suicide.

If there are three dimensions in us all, we must see

our lives in triplicate. There will be three kinds of prayer to fit our three dimensions, three kinds of silence, three ways of reading the Bible, three levels in making our confession, three types of sin. Part of the problem in the sacrament of penance has been the rolling of the three expressions of sin and sorrow into one.

Three seems to be the significant number, and yet no one has suggested that we are made up of three distinct persons on the pattern of the Holy Trinity. That there is a true reflection of the Godhead, I am certain, and no doubt we shall see the connection one day. At present we know ourselves to be each a single, individual person, living on three levels and showing three faces to those who know us best. Given a lampshade of three colors, the one bulb, viewed from different angles, may appear wholly blue, green, or red.

By far the most popular illustration of our makeup is taken from an actor on the stage. No theme in literature has proved more poignant than that of the clown, weary and brokenhearted, behind his grinning mask. As the experts tell us, the very word "person" derives from the masks used in Greek drama to disguise the face and to amplify the voice. Anyone who is able to grasp the difference between the person of the actor and the impersonation which he is performing comes very near to understanding the human mystery.

One point is now certain to me, that we all are actors; it is not a case of some being actors and others not. If men live "in three dimensions, the somatic, the mental, and the spiritual," then we may consider our powers of acting, on the somatic level first. Somatic means no more than the physical dimension in which our bodies strut upon the stage. In language, the active voice covers this operation in which we strive to reach the real physical world of people and to sell ourselves. Life on this level smacks of the footlights, for we are out to win an audience. We yearn to be noticed, to be heeded, to be applauded, to be loved. Dr. Sherwood Taylor used the label "Social Life" to describe our performance on life's stage. Over the years, such words as "society" and "social" have acquired a theatrical tang. At how many social gatherings we and others are busy acting, using a mask and giving an impersonation of ourselves.

It would be wrong to convey the impression that everyone in public is always artificial, always acting; nor is such acting always wrong. We were made that way and should recognize the fact. Yet it proves salutary from time to time and also amusing to look through our wardrobes, our jewel cases, and the cabinets in the bathroom jammed with toilet preparations to help us look our very best. Some among the moderns take equal trouble to make themselves always look their very worst. My act as a priest hardly requires your ties, cuff links, beards and mustaches for I must look holy at any cost. These are the trappings of actors and to them we add our wigs, medals, status symbols, and a script which includes name dropping, a witty sentence or two, and the very latest joke. I cease looking holy if another gets a laugh by telling my joke.

We may note in passing that religion also has a social level and a liturgy designed to be staged.

Shakespeare with "All the world's a stage" beautifully conveyed the lesson as, sixty years before him, did Sir Thomas More. More wrote:

> If you noticed that some silly actor was inordinately proud of wearing a golden coronet while taking the part of an Earl in a stage play, would you not laugh at his foolishness, knowing full well that when the play is

finished, he must put on his own shabby clothes and walk home in them? But don't you yourself also feel very smart and proud to wear an actor's outfit, forgetting that when your part is completed, you too will walk off the stage as poor as he? Nor do you care to note that your play may end just as soon as his.[4]

The poor actor returns home in his shabby clothes. As he leaves the stage and audience behind him, he retires to that second dimension in which men may express themselves. Dr. Frankl labels this the mental dimension. Sherwood Taylor calls it our private life. In language, this dimension is often covered by the passive voice, for we are no longer actively engaged in reaching others but sit back and let the world pour into us. This second dimension has a charm about it for those who love reading, music, color, nature, solitude, and thought.

At first sight, the tranquillity of the second dimension is due to the absence of an audience. We do what we want when we are alone. In the physical dimension we behave ourselves, for the curtain has risen and we must give an impersonation of ourselves. Once alone with the door shut, our consciousness is centered on ourselves. We live inside our heads. We relax, let our hair down, put our feet up and our teeth in a glass. William James said as much to the audience in Edinburgh at the start of his famous Gifford lectures; he began, "All of you sit here with a certain constraint because of the influence of the occasion," and went on to describe how different it would be if each listener was alone.

When alone many make a beeline for the phone. Others study the mirror in the hope that they look younger or for fear that they have cancer of the tongue. One friend confessed that he wrote furious let-

ters to the papers but had never posted one. Another
shyly showed me his conductor's baton: "Yes," said he,
"I switch on the radio every evening; I have longed to
conduct an orchestra all my life."

Anthony Trollope's glorious description of Archdeacon Grantly in his study, for me, gets near to the
bone:

> After breakfast, on the morning of which we are writ-
> ing, the archdeacon, as usual, retired to his study in-
> timating that he was going to be very busy, but that he
> would see Mr. Chadwick if he called. On entering this
> sacred room, he carefully opened the paper case on
> which he was wont to compose his favourite sermons,
> and spread on it a fair sheet of paper, and one partly
> written on; he then placed his inkstand, looked at his
> pen and folded his blotting paper; having done so, he
> got up again from his seat, stood with his back to the
> fire-place and yawned comfortably, stretching out vastly
> his huge arms and opening his burly chest. He then
> walked across the room and locked the door; and having
> so prepared himself, he threw himself into his easy
> chair, took from a secret drawer beneath his table a vol-
> ume of Rabelais, and began to amuse himself with the
> witty mischief of Panurge; and so passed the arch-
> deacon's morning on that day.[5]

Watching Archdeacon Grantly, we may ask ourselves
the question, are we entirely free of acting and self-im-
personation when we are alone? The very existence of
reflexive verbs in the structure of every language brings
out the duplicity which is ours. Such common expressions as "George fairly gave himself away," "She was
beside herself with anger," "I like my own company"
all suggest that two people, not one, inhabit our minds
and our rooms. One of the more frightening of such
expressions, "Pull yourself together," implies the con-

stant fear that we may lose our self-control. The very phrase "self-control" postulates a second person, another me in the driving seat. To soliloquize is to talk to yourself, and in this lies the genius of Shakespeare, for he could expose the duplicity of our second dimension on a first dimensional stage.

Few writers have better understood the problems of our second dimension than the great American psychologist William James. Of New England, Presbyterian stock—he once thought of joining the ministry—James suffered a nervous breakdown after completing his studies at the Harvard Medical School. Recovering completely from this dark night of the soul, he gave his life to the study of the causes of such mental and spiritual distress. He, who began so uncertainly, finished as one of the most tranquil and balanced personalities of his day. James was the first American to be invited to lecture in a European university and he chose for his Gifford lectures in Edinburgh "The Varieties of Religious Experience."

These lectures were published in a book which became a classic, one of the most helpful books that I have ever read. James did not invent the titles "Once-Born" and "Twice-Born" but he believed in the distinction and made it his own. So he opened his study of religion with an amusing lecture on the "Healthy-Minded," those simple, extrovert types who know no problem that cannot be cured by a dose of salts and a good stiff walk. Next, he introduces the "Twice-Born," introvert and full of doubts. For these much perplexity lies ahead. The naïve faith and practice of their childhood has to wither if they are to be born psychologically again. Undoubtedly James had suffered this himself. He illustrates the process in the stories of such great men as Luther, Tolstoy, Bunyan, Wesley, Robert

Louis Stevenson. Many of his sources, because of his own background, are Protestant. He himself belonged to no denomination, was well read in Catholic faith and practice, critical of certain saints who seemed to him narrow and stunted, in particular of St. Aloysius, St. Margaret Mary, and St. John of the Cross. He wrote warmly of the value of the Catholic confessional, and saw it as a great aid for the healthy-minded, who could thus shed their worries, clean the slate and start again.

I found James helpful especially in his eighth lecture on "The Divided Self." He took for granted as part of our psychological evolution the neurotic tensions which trouble many of us. The solution lies in accepting our makeup with its built-in duplicity. Life in this second dimension may prove full and rewarding but it may also bring acute distress. Drink, drugs, inferiority complexes, scruples, bouts of depression pertain to this dimension as, of course, do thoughts about suicide. Even when I am off stage and back in the greenroom, I still impersonate myself to myself.

Deeply religious people learn to accept the reality of a third dimension, the shadow of which is seen in our duplicity. For this reason Teresa of Ávila wrote of the higher part of the soul and the lower, and Thomas More knew a secret room within him, "the secret chamber of the mind, the privy-closet of the soul." Augustine tells us, "I carried my soul as if it were sliced in sunder and gored with blood and impatient even to be carried by me." Indeed, Augustine in his *Confessions* shows himself a master of this personal analysis and psychology. The duplicity inside himself both alarmed and tickled him. He was baffled to discover that a man may disobey himself. After a shrewd remark, "Ordinarily, indeed, a man does not laugh alone," he goes on to describe laughter on a lower level, when he had tricked his friends. "It was a delight and laughter which tickled us even to the very heart to think that we were deceiving those who feared no such thing of us."

Perhaps the most vivid account of the discovery of the third dimension was written by Alphonse Daudet and is quoted by William James:

> Homo Duplex; Homo Duplex. The first time that I perceived that I was two was at the death of my brother Henri, when my father cried out so dramatically, "He is dead, he is dead." While my first self wept, my second self thought, "How truly given was that cry, how fine it would be at the theatre." I was then fourteen years old.
>
> This horrible duality has often given me matter for reflection. Oh, this terrible second me, always seated while the other is on foot, acting, living, suffering, bestirring itself. This second me that I have never been able to intoxicate, to make shed tears or to put to sleep. And how it sees into things and how it mocks.[6]

Here Alphonse Daudet hits the nail squarely on the head. Such secret dissatisfaction with themselves, with their duplicity, corrodes many seemingly successful lives. The girl who has married well, the priest who is well received, the businessman who has done very well on the social level are, all too often, painfully ashamed of themselves. I myself have been astonished over the years at the number of those who socially love to brag about their successes, their humor, their many talents, but who in secret hate themselves. On his forty-fourth birthday, in his private diary, Evelyn Waugh touched on the three dimensions, but with no joy: "Guilt is beginning as my memory goes feeble. I am a very much older man than this time last year, physically infirm and lethargic. Mentally I have reached a stage of non-at-

tachment which if combined with a high state of
prayer (as it is not) would be edifying. I have kept
none of the resolutions made this day, a year ago. I
have vast reasons for gratitude and am seldom conscious of them."

For so many of us this innate duplicity wears us
down. We sweep the dust under the mat, lock the skel-
eton in the cupboard, drink and try to hide the bottles,
dodge every medical checkup, postpone, put off, com-
promise, cover up but with no hope of escape. We cry
out with Daudet, "Oh, this terrible second me," not
fully grasping that this second me is our very person,
yearning to break through the tissue of subterfuge.

The acceptance of dual personality and the effort to
recognize and respect the second me, who is always
mocking, in the end brings peace and stability. The
merit of William James lies in his willingness to admit
that the divided self is a normal stage in development.
Dr. Jung thought the same. In the book written shortly
before his death, Jung discussed this seeming division
in himself: "The play and counterplay between Personalities One and Two, which has run throughout my
life, has nothing to do with 'split' or dissociation in the
ordinary medical term. On the contrary, it is played
out in every individual." So we are not mad or schizo-
phrenic and once we face this division into two personalities, our problems are through. The wider the division between personalities One and Two, the greater
our sanity, the sharper our humor, for each personality
gains more room for maneuver, may stand back further
to see and to laugh at the other self.

Augustine solved his problem when he accepted the
third dimension and, of a sudden, found there his true
self. What he found in fact was his own free will. He
said to God, and I modernize the English, "What

drew me to your light was the recognition that I had a will of my own and of this I am as certain as that I am alive. When I chose anything or did not choose it, I knew for certain that it was I myself and no one else who made the choice; and I saw that in this lay the cause and root of my sin."[7]

So we come to the heart of the matter, the third dimension which so many philosophers, psychiatrists, poets, saints, mystics have tried to explain. For William James as, I think, for Fr. Teilhard de Chardin, our true Ego lives at the red-hot point of consciousness. Freud is also concerned with consciousness as an escape from repression and his will-to-pleasure principle examines the roots of sex. Dr. Frankl finds in the center of the heart a will-to-meaning; Dr. Tournier focuses on the person lying behind all the layers of impersonation, by which we give an imitation of the kind of person we think we ought to be.

We all are different in this third, spiritual dimension, for each human person is unique. I have derived the greatest help about our inner life not from William James, St. Teresa, Teilhard de Chardin but from a man who professed chemistry and who published several chemistry and general science textbooks for schools. Only at the end of his life did Dr. F. Sherwood Taylor write a book about religion, a slight volume of a hundred pages entitled *Two Ways of Life*. Other writers are neat, as was St. Teresa with her *Interior Castle*, or poetic as is Teilhard de Chardin, or academic with William James. Sherwood Taylor hits off exactly the delicacy, vagueness, and confusion at the very center of our hearts. Here is an uncharted region, swathed with clouds. When we think of examining our conscience, confessing sins, expressing sorrow, we need to make allowance for these clouds.

Dr. Sherwood Taylor's description has greatly helped me since 1947 when I read it first. I quoted it in an earlier book. Without apology I again repeat it to bring this complicated chapter to its close:

This inner life is lived in a strange enough world; for in truth each man and woman dwells in a different environment—so different that I believe that there are no two people who have so much as half in common. Men know each other's inner world so slightly that they neglect this difference and it is only when two people have a relation of utter love and trust that their inner lives begin to be perceptible to each other and are revealed as mutually most strange.

What are the constituents of this inner life? First there are memories of men and places and actions, a few pages curiously selected from countless volumes of experience—curiously selected and strangely distorted, as we find when old memories are confronted with the things remembered. There is a system, or at least a view of the world, constructed from principles whose origin is the thoughts and conclusions of ourselves and of others; whether known in the flesh or through their writings; some of these principles being casual and ill grasped sojourners, others smoothed and hardened by constant use into habits of thought and action. Memories and thoughts may be records of fact, or symbols of something within ourselves, or both of these; and always in the depth of the mind an unknown agent fashions for us symbols, fantasies and images which are manifest in dreams but also well up into and tinge the rational thoughts of our waking hours. All these are as it were the matter of the mind; but there are forces also—loves and hates, the magnetic drawing of the mind to beauty, truth, goodness, of the body to the objects of its desire. Above, within, beyond all these, we know the controlling I, who knows them, who knows that I can within ill-defined and uncertain limits choose what I shall think and what I shall do; Plato's charioteer driving his ill-matched team.

Perhaps deeper, or perhaps less clearly apprehended, are certain knowings which are not facts or yet desires, the knowing and turning to something that is changeless, that is not seen or heard by sense or imagination; something that remains when the tumult of the mind is hushed, when even the I is still and waiting. In this region there are no words, no images, but there is that to which every thought and fantasy and imagining and desire are subject.[8]

This may not describe your third dimension but it exactly covers mine and sets out the various layers of the third dimension unerringly. Let me set out the headings thus:

1 Curiously selected memories, often inaccurate.
2 A view of the world based on memories, conversations, books.
3 Habits of thought and action.
4 Dreams and fantasies which color rational thought.
5 The magnetic attraction of the mind to beauty, truth, goodness.
6 Of the body to the objects of its desire.
7 The capital "I," aware of its mastery and responsibility.
8 The yearning towards the changeless; not imaginable.
9 Absolute quiet in the awareness of that to which all thought is subject.

Religion and confession begin with points eight and nine of this catalogue. All the accounts of great conversions veer towards these two points. Dr. Tournier adds a third:

There is, also, an irresistible force within, which compels us to be honest to the bitter end, to throw off the mask of personage and uncover the person. When my

patient is in the throes of this struggle, his almost inau-
dible words are broken by long silences; there is taking
place within him another inner dialogue. This second
dialogue is with God, even if the man concerned is not
a believer and thinks he is only wrestling with himself.
His whole being resists as we all do; if he speaks it no
longer comes from himself but from a force more pow-
erful than he. The woman I mentioned who said "You
are implacable" was simply uttering aloud an answer
from her inner dialogue.[9]

When we speak of sin, sorrow, confession, a firm purpose of amendment, we are telling the truth but in
unreal, academic terms. Posturing on the human stage,
or worrying ourselves as actors in the greenroom we are
still impersonating and playing a part. Only in the
third dimension can we clowns get rid of our masks.

3—JESUS CHRIST, PSYCHIATRIST

No flippancy is intended when I call Christ a psychiatrist. The title is relevant today, exactly fits the gospel story and emphasizes the delicacy of that sacrament by which our sins are washed away.

Many other titles have been given to Christ: "Christ the King," "Jesus the Messiah," "Light of the World," "God Incarnate," but these have their roots in Scripture and theology. Thousands today, following in the footsteps of Nathanael and Nicodemus, are drawn to Christ through his authority. There are, however, thousands of others who remain unbelievers and yet are conscious of Christ's magnetic power. The title "Christ the Psychiatrist" preserves the reactions of those sick and sinful people in the gospel who knew nothing of other titles but were attracted by his understanding and sympathy. That little old lady who had suffered hemorrhage for years perhaps knew nothing of Jesus the Messiah but felt compelled to touch him in her misery.

In the sphere of psychology, Christ was some twenty centuries ahead of his day. His uncanny appreciation of human beings and their motivation gave him his mastery. Truths which he tossed off in a casual sentence would later be discovered by the experts and expanded into impressive tomes. For all our modern advances in psychotherapy, I sometimes wonder if we know as much about life's real problems as did those simple people listening to Christ in Galilee.

William James helps to illustrate this point with his collection of cases which record the varieties of religious experience. Perhaps two thirds of these hinge on a changing relationship with Jesus Christ. Centuries after his death, at the deepest level, he could bring peace and purpose to clever but unhappy men. What strange bedfellows were these? We find Luther and Augustine, Tolstoy and Wesley rubbing shoulders with that freethinking French Jew, M. Alphonse Ratisbonne. To synopsize Ratisbonne's account, he remarked in effect, later, "If anyone had said to me, 'Alphonse, in a quarter of an hour, you'll be adoring Jesus Christ as your God and Saviour,' I would have judged him mad."

The Christian mystics afford us a further illustration for, to judge from their spiritual writings, no two of them were anything like the same. To each his or her special vision, in that third dimension to which Christ so frequently referred. Deep in that misty world where resides the capital "I", each had a unique and personal experience and exchanged personal love. In the third dimension, all generalizations are invalid except one. The mystics had one common factor, a personal relationship with Christ. Otherwise, they differed greatly in style, emotion, imagination, environment, and thought. Thus St. Teresa of Ávila and St. John of the Cross were contemporaries and intimate friends, laboring in the same country and in the same religious order for the same reforms. Yet their contemplative lives, to judge by what they wrote, were entirely different. I once read in a learned journal how, when Teresa and John were in Toledo, Teresa, who had much trouble with prickly confessors, never thought of approaching her friend and fellow Doctor of the Church. Yet Teresa and John of the Cross are invariably grouped together; imagine the gap between this Spanish pair and Augustine, Bernard, De Caussade, Evelyn Underhill, Simone Weil, and Dag Hammarskjöld. In the third dimension, Christ fashioned a relationship with each individual through a person-to-person approach. Dr. Frankl, Dr. Tournier, and other great psychiatrists would agree that this is the only approach.

To appreciate Christ's technique and all that he added to man's yearning for forgiveness, it helps to consider what happened before his day. Man was there, sin was there, and guilt was there, all the world over, and in the most primitive forms of tribal worship there were penitential purifying rites. Sin in this primitive state was not personal but little more than an amalgam of magic and taboos. In much the same way as bad luck is predicted today for a man who is hardy enough to walk under a ladder, so in primitive days an arbitrary good or bad luck decided man's fate. He was a digit and could do nothing but seek outside help. So he invoked magic, and his confessor was the magician or the medicine man. We meet such magic in the Acts of the Apostles and vague traces of a primitive mentality survive in some Christian churches in our day.

The more sophisticated societies gradually freed themselves from the bonds of magic, and sin for these became the infringement of a code. Where more primitive people purged their sins in the first dimension by ritual washings, the philosophers retired to the second dimension with right reason as their guide. Sin was an offense against reason and the sinner could only kick himself for behaving like a fool. Here was the philosophy of doing the right thing, behaving sensibly, with all the discipline and self-denial which these demand. How greatly one must admire men of the caliber of Cicero, Seneca, the Emperor Marcus Aurelius, along

with their counterparts today. But a moral code based
on reason alone differs little from the code of conduct
taught by Victorian nannies and praised on Prize Days
by earnest headmasters in Victorian public schools. It
proves insufficient in the face of misery and guilt to
say, "I could kick myself, I have behaved badly, I have
let the side down, I am a something fool." Yet this
mentality is still met among Christian people for
whom the confessional box is a spiritual police court or
a psychiatrist's consulting room.

When we turn to the Old Testament, we discover a
far deeper appreciation of sin. We now have a personal
God, loving and paternal, in so many respects a patri-
arch. He made the laws as in the garden of Eden, gave
rewards and punishments. With the Old Testament,
love and sorrow entered religion; King David lay on
the ground weeping, where no tears of sorrow were
shed by Cicero. Yet despite such moving accounts of
sorrow and forgiveness, sin for the bulk of the Hebrew
people was a national, tribal transgression of the law.
The whole race had signed a covenant with God.
Moses was forever asking the people to be faithful, and
the high priest on the day of atonement prayed as
spokesman for the people, "O God, I have comitted
iniquity, transgressed and sinned before thee, I and my
house."

Some elements of these three attitudes to sin and
sorrow have survived. For some magic, in the form of
superstition, plays a part in the sacrament of penance,
for others sin, as a breach of the moral code, is shame-
ful while, for most Christians, a true sense of infidelity
has been borrowed from Old Testament times. The
whole approach to sin alters with the coming of Jesus
Christ. Yet Christ was emphatic that he had not come
to abolish the law of Moses but to fulfill it, and we
may ask ourselves how did he set about achieving this?

He did not amend the Mosaic law, as we may amend a constitution, nor did he tamper with ancient Hebrew liturgy. I would suggest that he fulfilled the law and brought it to life through his profound psychological insight of human needs. It may well be that such a revolutionary change demanded incarnation, for the person-to-person approach requires, at least in the beginning, a human being whom all can touch and hear and see.

To drive the point home, allow me to quote once more those lines by Dr. Sherwood Taylor which delineate the region in which Christ would work:

> This inner life is lived in a strange enough world; for in truth each man and each woman dwells in a different environment—so different that I believe that no two people have so much as half in common. Men know each other's inward world so slightly that they neglect the difference and it is only when two people have a relationship of utter love and trust that their inner lives begin to become perceptible to each other and are revealed as mutually most strange.

Such a barrier between persons is a commonplace of life and few manage to scale it; in the gospel story any such barrier is thrown up only by the sinner, never by Christ.

The first striking feature of Christ's method is his influence with the individual person, rarely with a crowd. He drew multitudes but somehow failed to hold them and he had only a handful of faithful friends around him when he died. The crowds wanted to make him king for the wrong reasons; they followed him only for signs and wonders and, to use his own expression, "were dull of heart." Even the enthusiasm generated on Palm Sunday could not last five days. I see a mystery here. Where the Holy Spirit after Pentecost inspired mass conversions, Christ never did. As

John reports at the start of Christ's crusade, "While he was in Jerusalem for the feast, there were many who came to believe in his name seeing the miracles that he did. But Jesus would not give them his confidence; he had knowledge of them all and did not need assurances about any man because he could read men's hearts."[1]

What was so unusual about Christ's method? I would say his third dimensional approach. For him it was the person, not the various impersonations, which counted most. He knew all about the divided self, the sick soul, man's search for meaning, the very subjects about which our modern psychiatrists write. Christ reached the clown behind the mask. Surely it was this sympathy and understanding that gave him so many personal relationships. He treated each individual differently. Thus he appreciated the fear of the Pharisee Nicodemus, frightened for his reputation, and hence calling on Jesus after dark. This to Christ was genuine, not play-acting like the hospitality of Simon, another Pharisee. Simon's impersonation was brushed aside, but the tears of the prostitute who gate-crashed the party were accepted as sincere. At the very moment when Pontius Pilate was preparing to condemn him, Christ informed this well-intentioned pagan that his was the lesser sin. Peter had publicly denied his master; it took one glance, not to deflate but to forgive him, with the relief of bitter tears.

In one of the most pithy of his parables about sin, Christ showed how little he was fooled by play-acting, how greatly he loved those who were sincere. The Pharisees had been murmuring about the company he kept and Christ threw up a question, his frequent and favorite technique:

"Tell me what you think; there was a man who had two sons and when he went up to the first and said, 'Away with thee, my son and work in my vineyard today,' he answered, 'Not I,' but he relented afterwards and went. Then he went up to the other and said the like to him and his answer was 'I will, Sir' but he did not go. Which of these two carried out his father's will?" "The first," they said. And Jesus said to them, "Believe me, the publicans and harlots are further on the road to God's kingdom than you."

I love this parable for the boy who said "No" on his first and second dimensions said "Yes" in his heart.

I am unable to think of any other philosopher, statesman, religious leader who based every judgment on one virtue only, sincerity. In the gospel, nothing is made of looks, wealth, intellectual talents, past reputations, good or bad. The original twelve certainly were unreliable, boastful, intolerant, doubting; one proved insincere. Peter was cowardly on one fatal occasion and a curious hesitancy continued throughout his life. St. Paul rebuked him for it and in the old, old story of *Quo Vadis?* Christ confronted a Peter running away from martyrdom. Yet Peter was offered a different chance and took it by the lakeside: when Christ asked him three times, "Simon, son of John, do you love me?" the apostle worded the most sincere prayer ever expressed. "Peter was upset that he asked him a third time, 'Do you love me?' and said, 'Lord, you know everything; you know I love you,'" invoking Christ's own knowledge as his proof. Had he said these words, "You know I love Christ," to James or John they might well have hesitated; they might have said, "You denied that you knew him only this day last week." Because Christ knew all Peter's weaknesses, he also knew the truth.

Dr. Tournier quotes a penetrating statement by a French doctor: "A complete confession is always necessary in medicine." The same is certainly true with Christ. And the answer to Addison's gibe that the act of contrition of a hypocrite is itself hypocritical is surely to be found in Peter's prayer.

Christ's preoccupation with sincerity is underlined in all his dealings with the Pharisees. Not all the Pharisees were bad. Many later became disciples and three were noble, Nicodemus, Gamaliel, and the "Pharisee of Pharisees," the great St. Paul. The fault of the Pharisees was to center their lives in the wrong dimension and to seek the applause of men. Christ himself, so severe in his criticism of their behavior, never denied their righteousness. He told his disciples, "Let your righteousness exceed the righteousness of the scribes and Pharisees," to which John Wesley added a shrewd rider, "Before we inquire how our righteousness may exceed theirs, let us examine whether at present we come up to it."

Consider the Pharisee who was praying in the temple, externally on every count a good man. He lived chastely, never cheated his neighbor, gave alms generously, and fasted twice a week. Had the temple had its confessional box, he would have been scratching his head and puzzling what to confess. But I suspect that he would have made a confession frequently to edify others and to create a good effect. His one mistake was a common one of living in the first dimension and acting his faith on the stage. He was, in fact, an actor giving a brilliant impersonation of a holy man. Actors and actresses often remark how they perform better if they believe in the part that they are asked to play. Our Pharisee believed in his part, he loved the law, the liturgy, Sabbath day observance, was proud of his vocation and welcomed the self-discipline which it entailed. His only fault was the desire to be clapped. The Pharisees, as Christ told the people, prayed to be seen praying, fasted to look austere, gave

alms in public to get their names on to every worthwhile subscription list.

Christ asked of his disciples the opposite. They were
to pray in secret, to disguise their fasting, to give alms
in private so that they could burrow downwards to the
third dimension to become and to be themselves. On
these precise points, how many of us take Christ's injunctions seriously? If we do not, then we too are
phony and our prayer is one that thanks God that we
are not hypocrites like this Pharisee. I feel for that
poor Pharisee. I remember the days when we young
priests were urged to be edifying, to be seen praying by
our congregations, to live austerely at least when any of
the laity were round about. How many devout Christian parents put on an act to edify the children or the
priest.

I know nothing about you, but I myself cannot recall a moment in my life when I could not say with St.
Peter, "Lord, you know everything, you know I love
you," but with a condition attached. When I examine
that word "everything" and break it down, then my
prayer takes on a sincere but side-splitting contradiction. "Lord, because you know my hypocrisies, you
know I love you" is about the most honest prayer that
man can voice.

When the elders complained that Christ's disciples
ate food without a ritual washing, he answered with
words from Isaiah, "This people honors me with their
lips but their heart is far from me." Here, the third dimension is divided from the others and here, too, we
meet Christ's deep psychological use of the word
"heart."

In very form of language, the heart has been used to
pinpoint the center of our being and it has been
honored as the seat of all emotions, more especially of

love. For a great many people today the heart has become the symbol for physical love, for sex, for that sensuous, sentimental emotion about which we hear in every second pop song, and at which we gaze yearly as St. Valentine's feast comes round. For some unexplained reason, the heart covers a boy and girl who are dating but not a young mother fondling her baby, who must make do with a diaper instead.

A similar maudlin use of the heart is found in religious language and devotional art. Christ himself was the victim of such emotionalism in certain epochs, especially in connection with the seventeenth-century devotion to the Sacred Heart. An understanding of Christ's use of the word "heart," an appreciation of his psychotherapy, might have spared us much embarrassment and the imagery of Guido Reni and Holman Hunt. A beautiful picture may also be untrue to life. I find nowhere in the gospel, or in St. Paul, any justification of that sentimentality which, in my boyhood, passed for piety. When Christ used the word "heart" he was always down to earth and, like any good doctor, both gentle and tough.

He used the word "heart" often, but always to indicate the third, spiritual dimension, incoherent, swathed in mist. Language itself gives to the word a profound, psychological meaning which may be expressed as "the real person" or "the real me." We speak of the purehearted, hardhearted, brokenhearted and Christ did the same. Thus the Pharisee who went to the temple "made this prayer in his heart, 'I thank thee God that I am not as other men.' " There was no acting, no impersonation, but a genuine, deep-seated superiority complex in this prayer. Again, Christ said of the Pharisees, "They have set their hearts on high places," and to them, "Why do you murmur in your hearts?" The same man who said, "A man who lusts after a woman in his heart has already committed adultery," remarked to the bystanders, "Learn of me for I am meek and humble of heart."

When you think of it, the heart may be good, bad, or indifferent but it is always genuine. In a heart-to-heart talk both parties mean what they say. If we say that Fred is eating his heart out, we mean that his frustrations, desires, heartaches are driving him to despair. To be of good heart implies a deep determination, to lose heart is to throw up everything. Finally we reach the heart of the matter and Jesus Christ, psychiatrist.

With the utmost sympathy and understanding, Christ peels away all layers of sham. First, with unusual emphasis, he stated categorically that evil does not come to us from outside. The audience was sufficiently puzzled for Christ to repeat the statement three times. After so many centuries of magic and taboos, the outward observance of rules and regulations, men could not grasp that they generate good and evil within themselves.

The scene is an impressive one, for Christ first turned on the Pharisees who had been secretly grumbling because the disciples had broken with tradition and eaten without first washing their hands. Christ in answer quoted Isaiah about lip service and made it clear that no food, washed or unwashed, is able to defile a man.

Next, he turned to the people, exclaiming, "Hear me all of you and understand; there is nothing outside a man which by going into him can defile him; but the things that come out of man are what defile him." Thus, at a stroke, he broke the tyranny of tradition and taboos.

Leaving the crowd and entering a house, he found the disciples puzzled and anxious to question him. "And he said to them, 'Then you are also without understanding? Do you not see, whatever goes into a man from outside cannot defile him since it enters not his heart but his stomach and so passes on? For, within, out of the heart of man come evil thoughts, fornication, theft, murder, adultery, deceit, licentiousness, envy, slander, pride, foolishness. All these evil things come from within and they defile a man.' "

Let me quote again, "A complete confession is always necessary in medicine," for this was the point towards which Christ had to work. He is scotching forever those two deceits mentioned by C. S. Lewis which enable us to kid ourselves indefinitely with "My heart is in the right place" and "I would not hurt a fly." Sooner or later we are driven back into a corner, we are forced to admit that, at the very center of our being, we are schemers, capable of every kind of underhand method to get what we want. Christ put this in one neat sentence, "Where your treasure is, there will your heart be too."

Christ knew men so well and loved them so much and treated each with so much sympathy and understanding that he drew from the sinners in the gospel that genuine confession which alone could bring them happiness. No force, physical or moral, was ever used. Christ never asked anyone to confess. He infused such confidence through his kindness that sinners came to him. His friends in the gospel had one mark in common, not innocence, not righteousness but spontaneous, homemade sincerity.

Christ returned to the theme of the heart on many occasions, not to find fault, to threaten, or to bluster but to teach men to know and to help themselves. Perhaps the most subtle of his psychological lessons turns on a fruit tree and its fruit. He said, "No good tree bears bad fruit nor again does a bad tree bear good fruit. Each tree is known by its fruit . . . The good man out of the good treasure of his heart produces good, and the evil man out of his evil treasure produces evil; for out of the abundance of the heart, the mouth speaks."

I remarked earlier how Christ would toss off a casual sentence which centuries later the experts would expand into tomes. This phrase "out of the abundance of the heart, the mouth speaks" may serve as an example for it forms the substance of many psychology books today. Christ's famous dictum is variously translated and we may take our pick. The more traditional renderings tell us that it is from the fullness, the abundance, the overflow of the heart that the mouth speaks. The Jerusalem Bible turns it the other way round: "For a man's words flow out of what fills his heart." As a onetime schoolmaster I wince at one translation only; no boy in my class would have written "A man's mouth speaks what his heart is full of" and got away with it.

Whatever the translation, Christ's thought is clear. Good and evil are brewed in the third dimension and work their way outwards in thoughts and words and deeds. From the heart, my true desires, good or bad, will overflow into the other dimensions to affect not just thoughts and words but my voice, reading, haberdashery, friends, tastes, jokes. The very impersonations which I stage on the other levels are programed in the heart.

Dr. Viktor Frankl, in *The Doctor and the Soul*, sums up the theories about human motivation put forward by modern psychiatrists:

Psychoanalysis speaks of the *pleasure principle*, individual psychology of the *status drive*. The pleasure principle might be termed the *Will-to-pleasure*; the status drive is equivalent to the *Will-to-power*. But where do we hear of that which most deeply concerns man; where is the innate desire to give as much meaning as possible to one's life, to actualize as many values as possible— what I should like to call the *Will-to-meaning?* This *Will-to-meaning* is the most human phenomenon of all since an animal certainly never worries about the meaning of its existence. Yet psychotherapy would turn this *Will-to-meaning* into a human frailty, a neurotic complex. A therapist who ignores man's spiritual side and who is thus forced to ignore the *Will-to-meaning* is giving away one of his most valuable assets. For it is to this will that a psychotherapist should appeal. Again and again we have seen that an appeal to continue life, to survive the most unfavorable conditions can be made only when such a survival appears to have a meaning. That meaning must be specific and personal, a meaning which can be realized by this one person alone. For we must never forget that every man is unique in the universe.[2]

Now Dr. Frankl is one of the leading international psychiatrists and when he asks, "Where do we hear of that which most deeply inspires man?" and fails to find an answer in his own profession, he should turn to the gospel for relief. Christ, in a passage already quoted, listed the evils which flow from the heart of man. Deep in the third dimension, you do not find this specific sin or that one but the will-to-pleasure which will overflow into the other dimensions as fornication, adultery, licentiousness. Nor do you find in the heart any specific sin of greed but the will-to-power which will be manufactured into slander, envy, pride, murder, theft. But what of the will-to-meaning? This too is fully illustrated in the gospel in the case of those poor sinners who were drawn to Christ. He put meaning into their lives—the aim of Dr. Frankl also—for which reason I call my chapter "Jesus Christ, psychiatrist."

4—THANK YOU, EVE

In a book about confession, dare one omit all reference to Adam and Eve? They started it. This endearing pair, so easily identified by their very lack of clothing, have been with us since our tenderest years. In childhood we were told about them and could see them being driven from the garden in our picture books. We were probably too young to appreciate that, when they first donned clothing, they began both man's first impersonation and first coverup.

There is no way of escaping from Adam and Eve. Visit any art gallery and there they will be, looking slightly sheepish; go to a night club and you should hear a joke about them, listen to a sermon and, sooner or later, the preacher will round on the hapless pair. Women may forget Eve but we men cannot get rid of Adam; we carry a chunk of his apple in our throats.

The story of Adam and Eve is, surely, one of the greatest ever told. It does not lose its magic because some progressive people label it a myth. A few of the details about the garden of Eden come under fire from botanists, paleontologists, geographers, and Women's Lib. Not a few Christians, on the defensive, feel that the story may be accepted only as legend or allegory. Such labels as allegory, legend, myth turn the tale of Adam and Eve into a fairy story, not to be taken too seriously.

Frankly, the use of such labels in no way destroys the truth of the story for me; allegory, poetry, history, myth are legitimate forms of revelation with the will-to-meaning as our goal. A historian myself, by taste and training, I find more truth in *Hamlet, Animal Farm,* or *Don Quixote* than in Lord Macauley's or Winston Churchill's history books. Why doubt the veracity of Genesis? Here we have one of the oldest stories in the world, recorded in detail by primitive people with a depth and subtlety rarely if ever achieved since. Further, without the fall of Adam and Eve we are doomed to live without meaning; lastly, it just so happens that we may check the truth of the story for ourselves.

We all know, by direct experience in our third dimension, that we have a fatal flaw within ourselves. When I say or think to myself, "Hang it all, I'm only human," I am using Adam and Eve as my excuse. Is there anyone who would not admit in his search for meaning that there are endless situations in which he dare not trust himself? Many of these are trivial. After a family squabble about washing-up, a teenage boy shouted hysterically to his mother, "You are acting like a typical teenager," and, as she added in a letter to me, "I certainly was." A dear old priest, long dead, used to put it sweetly, mumbling, "Lord, why did you make me such a bloody fool?" under what he thought, mistakenly, was his breath. The acceptance of such a flaw in ourselves becomes easier as we grow older, for the memory of past scenes, deceits, humiliations teaches us to tolerate ourselves.

No modern book helps more to link Adam's sin to our own search for meaning than William Golding's *Lord of the Flies.* Others must have found the same, for this best seller went through thirteen reprints in thirteen years. A review in the London *Times* hit off exactly the moral of this devastating story, the spiritual collapse of those well-intentioned, nicely mannered, intelligent children, cut off without adult supervision, on a desert isle. Having taught boys of that very age, I could see my own little darlings behaving in the exact way that the author described. The review in the *Times* opens: "Mr. Golding knows exactly what boys are like; he has a compelling imagination and the vivid realism with which he describes the disintegration of their untried and precarious civilisation under the pressure of raw nature carries the reader to the bloody climax; a most absorbing and instructive tale."

Whether or not we label *Lord of the Flies* as myth or fable, it is exactly true to life. When those decent, innocent boys were left on their own, the will-to-pleasure and the will-to-power prevailed. When these led the pack to cruelty, greed, lust, fear, guilt, superstition, the only two boys who retained a will-to-meaning broke down in despair:

> Piggy took off his glasses, plainly troubled, "I dunno Ralph," he said, "We just got to go on, that's all. That's what the grown-ups would do . . . What makes things break up as they do?"[1]

Poor cross-eyed Piggy, blind without his glasses, was the one hero in the story; as anyone would guess who thinks of Good Friday, he paid for his honesty with his life. When the navy had arrived and the ragamuffins had come slinking from the woods to safety, the officer in charge saw Ralph. "In the middle of them, with filthy body, matted hair and unwiped nose, Ralph wept for the end of innocence, the darkness of man's heart and the fall through the air of the true, wise friend called Piggy."

The flaw in man, here played out by boys to the shame of Ralph and Piggy, has led many intelligent men and women to despair of the human race. As

Thomas Hobbs put it, "The life of man is solitary, poor, nasty, brutish and short." Readers of my age have lived through two world wars and the slaughter of twenty million people; the exact figure is anybody's guess. Wars, sadism, lust, greed, money-grabbing induce in many a cynicism which burrows to our very roots. In answer to Piggy's query, "What makes things break up as they do?" we would all say: the selfishness of man. And the kernel of such an answer would carry us back to the Pharisee praying in the temple, "I thank thee, Lord, that I am not as other men."

A surprisingly large number of people today, each modestly admitting that he or she is different, would accuse mankind of letting the world down. Dear little old ladies feeding the birds, devoted housewives queuing for pet foods in the supermarket, ecologists with fanatical fire in their eyes, nature lovers, may well prefer animals to men. Once, at a private meeting which started in a friendly fashion, I was astonished to discover that thirteen people out of sixteen thought that animals were better than men. Walt Whitman in a celebrated passage expressed such an attitude well:

> I could turn and live with animals, they are so placid and self-contained.
> I stand and look at them, long and long.
> They do not sweat and whine about their condition.
> They do not lie awake in the dark and weep for their sins.
> Not one is dissatisfied, not one is demented with the mania for owning things.
> Not one kneels to another, nor to his kind that lived thousands of years ago.
> Not one is respectable or unhappy over the whole earth.

In theory, no Christian could accept so gloomy a view. Optimism is, surely, essential to a faith based on the gospel—the very word gospel means good news. In her early decades the Church was optimistic; despite unending persecution, Peter and Paul were happy and hopeful men. Augustine admitted his sins but his sorrow was never morbid; his *Confessions* are not chiefly concerned with his failings but proclaim God's loving-kindness towards him. The lovely old Easter hymn, the "Exultet," gives Adam and Eve their acquittal and describes their fall as a "happy fault." So much for the theory but, when it comes to practice, Christians have proved as gloomy as the rest.

Here is a contradiction for which I can find no answer; an inconsistency which Christian pessimists need to correct. It is difficult to ignore the note of gloom struck by so many orators and writers in the various branches of the Christian faith. The variety of religious experience has proved to be a variety of fears and scruples, panic about salvation, threats of damnation, a morbid preoccupation with men's sins. How explain such a Dismal Desmond approach? Was too much attention paid to the apocalyptic passages in the Scriptures; were the prophets of gloom themselves passing through a time of crisis; or could it be that the great revivalists discovered, as the journalists have later, that crowds turn out to hear bad news? Whatever the reasons, in certain epochs the emphasis was on punishment for sinners, on all that is wrong with the world. The picture of George Fox tramping the streets and crying aloud, "Woe to the bloody city of Lichfield," is no caricature.

Last year, in Washington, D.C., I shook hands with the distinguished Capuchin, Father Sebastian, whose lectures have been delighting thousands over many years. Indeed, I sought him out after American friends, living in Britain, had told me of the benefit they had derived from a course of lectures entitled "What Is Right with the World." Father Sebastian drew this happy approach from the right sources, the books and verses of G. K. Chesterton.

Chesterton was by temperament an optimist. Once, years ago, a Portuguese doctor who was driving me to Fatima gave me a quotation which I have never been able to trace. Braking his car vigorously in a narrow lane, my friend remarked with due solemnity, "As your Mr. Chesterton said, 'An optimist guesses right as often as a pessimist but he is much happier.'"

Chesterton, however, was not just a cheery soul who viewed the world through rosy glasses; he was, among modern writers, the supreme theological optimist. In a poem entitled "The Pessimist" he fills up the verses with the joy of the incarnation but begins and ends brusquely:

> You, that have snarled through the ages, take your answer and go—I know your hoary question, the riddle that all men know.[2]

The charm of Chesterton's optimism lies in his forthright acceptance of sin. He was humble enough not to be surprised by his weakness or to attribute the blame to other agencies. We often attempt this. We complain about our heredity, environment, teachers, clergy, doctors, even our psychiatrists. "You are responsible; you gave me the excuse for behaving badly," wrote an angry patient to her psychotherapist. Chesterton was very happy to blame only himself. On the very day when he was received into the Catholic Church and at the moment when he was making his first confession, a friend, waiting for him in another room, scribbled on a piece of paper, "He joined the Church to restore his innocence. Sin was almost the greatest reality to him.

He became a Catholic because of the Church's practical power in dealing with sin."

The wisdom and insight of G.K.C. is seen in his whole-hearted acceptance of sin as inevitable in man. Here for him was both tragedy and triumph, the risk that had to be taken, the pain that had to be suffered for the greatest experiment known in our creation, man's freedom of choice. Evolution was less to the fore in Gilbert Keith Chesterton's day. All the advances in this field should have thrilled him, for evolution adds to the story of Adam and Eve a more profound meaning at the moment when the last of the hominoids reached that point of consciousness when it could stand back, judge a situation, and choose for itself. The first free creatures on earth made the wrong decision, but Chesterton saw in this a profound advance. He wrote of Adam:

> When Adam went from Paradise,
> He saw the sword and ran;
> The dreadful shape, the new device,
> the pointed end of Paradise,
> And saw what Peril is, and Price
> And knew he was a man.

Many have said as much before, nor is this the whole story, but Chesterton had a unique, intuitive, and penetrating point of view. Some would see him as an uncanonized saint, all who know his works would accept that he was a mystic, a point brought out by his dear friend Maisie Ward in her great biography. His preoccupation was with the fall of man and the challenge behind it, leading to a second Adam, the Son of God made man.

I was pleased that Maisie Ward judges as "one of his most brilliant illustrations" a passage of his which helped me much in my schoolboy days. We may speak, says G.K.C., of a manly man but not of a whaley whale. "If you want to dissuade a man from drinking his tenth whisky, you slap him on the back and say, 'Be a man.' No one who wishes to dissuade a crocodile from eating his tenth explorer would slap it on the back and say, 'Be a crocodile.' For we have no notion of a perfect crocodile; no allegory of a whale expelled from his whaley Eden." This passage if taken seriously, and it is very serious, would give us the answer to Walt Whitman's gloomy verdict on mankind. For we have an image of a perfect man and the chance to attain it and the power to pick the means to achieve this end. Animals commit no sin but they have no higher standards, no will-to-meaning, no personal goal.

I must have been ten years old when I first saw G. K. Chesterton in the Church of Our Lady of Victories, High Street, Kensington. My father took me into this old church to pray and as we walked up the side aisle to the Lady Chapel, he tapped my shoulder and whispered in my ear. I gathered that I was not to stare or to turn round quickly but that there was a very famous man just behind me on a chair. I would like to tell you that he was wearing his cape and his curious pince-nez, but memory is deceitful after fifty years. This I recall, that the chair looked small and the occupant enormous and that if he had not been frowning, I would have judged that he was asleep. Dates are now hazy but I would guess that Chesterton became a Catholic some two years later and very soon afterwards wrote his *Orthodoxy*. Maybe it was the plan for this which made him frown.

Maisie Ward maintains that *Orthodoxy* is by far the most personal of Chesterton's writings, that it is "his history of his own mind." That it is a remarkable and most encouraging book, I agree after several readings, and would recommend it to anyone in search of meaning who finds himself bogged down. One particular passage deserves particular attention because it answers poor Piggy's question, "What makes things break up as they do?" Indeed, in a paragraph or two, Chesterton explains the flaw in Adam and Eve, deals with the Pharisee praying in the temple, begins to emphasize the importance of confession, and reveals unwittingly both his optimism and his humility. For me, this passage brings back nostalgic memories of the London of my boyhood, when Hanwell enjoyed a peculiar reputation thanks to its enormous mental home. Chesterton's second chapter, "The Maniac," opens thus:

> Thoroughly worldly people never understand even the world; they rely altogether on a few cynical maxims which are not true. Once, I remember walking with a prosperous publisher who made a remark which I had often heard before; it is, indeed, almost a motto of the modern world. Yet I had heard it once too often and I saw suddenly that there was nothing in it. The publisher said of somebody, "That man will get on; he believes in himself." And I remember that as I lifted my head to listen, my eye caught an omnibus on which was written "Hanwell." Said I to him, "Shall I tell you where the men are who believe most in themselves? For I can tell you. I know of men who believe in themselves more colossally than Napoleon or Caesar. I know where flames the fixed star of certainty and success, I can guide you to the thrones of the Supermen. The men who really believe in themselves are all in lunatic asylums."

> He said mildly that there were a good many men after all who believed in themselves and were not in lunatic asylums. "Yes, there are," I retorted, "and you of

all men ought to know them. That drunken poet from whom you would not take a dreary tragedy, he believes in himself. That elderly minister with an epic from whom you were hiding in a back room, he believes in himself. If you consulted your business experience instead of your ugly, individualistic philosophy, you would know that believing in himself is one of the commonest signs of a rotter. Actors who can't act believe in themselves; and debtors who won't pay. It would be much truer to say that a man will certainly fail because he believes in himself. Complete self-confidence is not merely a sin; complete self-confidence is a weakness. Believing utterly in one's self is an hysterical and superstitious belief like believing in Joanna Southcote; the man who has it, has Hanwell written on his face as plain as it is written on that bus."

And to all this my friend, the publisher, made this very deep and effective reply: "Well, if a man is not to believe in himself, in what is he to believe?" After a long pause, I replied, "I will go home and write a book in answer to that question." This is the book that I have written in answer to it.

G. K. Chesterton wrote his book and lived his life to combat the one, insidious, psychological heresy, practiced by those who believe in themselves. Adam and Eve were the first, followed by billions, including King David, the Pharisee in the temple, Judas Iscariot, the prep school kids on a desert island, Adolf Hitler, you and me. G. K. Chesterton delighted in man's basic weakness, for he knew that those who stand on their own two feet are heading for disaster; every idol has feet of clay. St. Paul said as much. Writing to the Corinthians, the apostle recognized the danger of pride. To keep him from believing in himself, God had given him "a thorn in the flesh," a chronic debility, which the experts have interpreted differently. Paul carried with him throughout his life some physical or moral weakness, impurity, epilepsy, anxiety: the nature of this thorn is anybody's guess but the purpose of such a trial Paul well understood. "About this thing, I have pleaded with the Lord three times for it to leave me but he said, 'My grace is enough for you; my power is at its best in weakness.' So I shall be very happy to make my weaknesses my special boast so that the power of Christ may stay over me and that is why I am quite content with my weaknesses and with the insults, hardships, persecutions and the agonies I go through for Christ's sake. For when I am weak, then I am strong."

Though he probably never guessed it, G. K. Chesterton had the good news of the gospel woven into the fabric of his mind. In a truly Christian style he denounced the hypocrites, the do-gooders, the people who believed in themselves. He said to them and especially to one of them, "Chuck it, Smith." But if he attacked the establishment men, the puritans, the self-righteous, he did this to defend the dignity and freedom of those who did not believe in themselves. So he loved the people who had not spoken and the rolling English drunkard who made the rolling English road. It was typical of G. K. Chesterton to write a poem in honor of dust and to end it with this triumphant stanza:

> When God to all his Paladins
> By his own splendour swore
> To make a fairer face than heaven
> of dust and nothing more.

Shortly before his death, Chesterton came upon T. S. Eliot's "The Hollow Men." In this he read of the deep and morbid pessimism of the newer generation, expressed in the lines

> This is the way the world ends,
> This is the way the world ends,
> This is the way the world ends,
> Not with a bang but a whimper.

After reading this Chesterton wrote: "Forgive me if I say in my old-world fashion that I am damned if I ever felt like that . . . I knew that the world was perishable and would end but I did not think that it would end with a whimper but, if anything, with a trump of doom. I will even be so indecently frivolous as to burst into song and say to the young pessimist:

> Some sneer; some snigger; some simper;
> In the youth where we laughed and sang.
> And *they* may end with a whimper,
> But *we* will end with a bang."

Maisie Ward who knew G.K. so well ends her biography with this detail and sums up his ambitions thus: "His last message for this generation was the sound of the trumpet calling us to Resurrection. A dead world must find life again, must go back to the meaning of Genesis." It is because this great man gave Adam and Eve their due, saw the dignity of man in his very weakness that I have given him a place of honor in this book.

5—SHOW ME THE WAY TO GO HOME

We may miss the point of Christ's story if we call it the parable of the prodigal son.[1] In the first place, Christ was not drawing our attention to the boy but to his father; secondly, this son was a wastrel and prodigal only in the uncomplimentary use of that word. Thanks to the parable, the word "prodigal" has come to mean repentant and this the boy in the parable never was. Preachers and hymn-writers often harp on the deep sorrow of the prodigal but this the boy himself never expressed.

Do you remember that famous old hymn which we used to sing at parish missions:

> God of mercy and compassion,
> Look with pity upon me;
> Father, let me call Thee Father,
> 'Tis Thy son returned to Thee.

It was a good hymn, but one thing is certain, the prodigal son did not sing it as he set out on his return journey; his mood would have been better covered by "Show Me the Way to Go Home." As St. Luke tells us, he came to his senses by the pigsties and his sorrow amounted to no more than this: "How many of my father's paid servants have more food than they want and here I am dying of hunger."

Too much emphasis on the sorrow of the son obscures the vital lesson which Christ was trying to teach. This parable is of unique importance, for only one man in history had the knowledge and authority sufficient to attempt such a comparison. I see no reason why others could not have thought out some other of Christ's parables, the sower, for example, or the good Samaritan. Teresa of Avila, Thomas More, C. S. Lewis, and other imaginative writers produced excellent parables in their day. But when it comes to sin, even the holiest of the saints would know only the sinner's reactions and maybe this is why the prodigal son has been treated so well. One man alone had firsthand knowledge of God's reactions to the sinner and his sin. In this parable, more than in any other, we acquire an insight into God's line of thought.

The story of the prodigal son is grouped with two others, for Christ thought the moral so important that he repeated it three times. And he began with a simple human instinct, known to all his listeners, to reveal, of a sudden, that such a reaction is also divine. How astonishing to invite a crowd of sinful people to examine their own feelings if they want to know God's attitude to those who have sinned. He began by asking, "What man among you?" before describing the behavior of the shepherd who leaves ninety-nine sheep in the wilderness because he discovers that one has strayed. He would not have put the question, had he not known that every farmer in the audience would have done the same.

While the farmers pondered the thought, he turned to the women: "What woman with ten drachmas would not, if she lost one, light a lamp and sweep out the house and search thoroughly until she found it? And then when she found it, call together her friends and neighbors: 'Rejoice with me,' she would say, 'I have found the drachma I lost.'"

This method of teaching a vital lesson proves especially effective, for we have each experienced such a reaction in ourselves. Few of us now deal with sheep or share the shepherd's anxiety, but many of us have our pets. Recently I had to recall the woman who dropped the drachma, for I mislaid the cap of my fountain pen. Others joined me in the search out of kindness with an enthusiasm much less than my own. The cap could not be found and a neighbor offered me another, for he had two. I thanked him without saying that I did not really want his cap but my own. Eventually we called the search off, I persuading myself that the lost cap was old and battered and that I rarely used that pen anyway. When the searchers had all left and I was ready for bed, I began the hunt again. I pulled out the furniture, turned out my pockets, searched every drawer. No doubt the psychiatrists have a name for the compulsion which drives an elderly priest in his pajamas to rummage in the garbage cans in the middle of the night. Does it sound fanciful to suggest that, in the back of the mind, there lurks a personal sense of duty towards anything that belongs to me?

So the fountain pen cap was retrieved soon after midnight and I slept peacefully. Indeed, my first thoughts on waking were not for God or myself but for the miscreant top. I experienced real joy and satisfaction in having saved it but, after so much fuss, I have to chuckle, for I have not used that pen since.

Presumably, you are not so nutty but you may have experienced the same. In all cases of loss, it pays to analyze one's feelings, for it was to these that Christ appealed in his effort to tell us about God. Simone Weil, who makes her points with the fewest number of words, has this to say in her comments on the *Paternoster:* "He is Our Father; there is nothing real in us which does not come from Him. We belong to Him. He loves us since He loves Himself and we are His."[2]

Here, surely, is the exact truth, the theme that lies

behind the incarnation, the key point, the only point in these three parables. Admittedly it takes some swallowing. Theologians and philosophers agree that if there is a supreme being, he must *be* supreme. Were God to lack anything, he would have to surrender his divinity. How can he need or yearn for me? Yet here we have Christ, in three precise parables, teaching what seems to be the opposite. Christ attributes to the infinite God the very sentiments of the housewife sweeping her house, of the shepherd searching for his sheep, of myself in pajamas at midnight sifting the garbage for the top of my fountain pen. Could we solve the problem by presuming in God those three dimensions which we have in ourselves? May we say that God does not need us but he does want us; this was the situation of the father in the story of the prodigal son?

Christ's three stories are carefully graded to bring out the three situations in which a man wants his own. The coin was an inanimate object, the errant sheep had movement and was stupid, the prodigal, when he set out to waste his father's money, chose such a course deliberately.

It would be foolish to attempt a comment on this famous story in so short a space. It is, however, important to study the psychology of a sinner and, as one modern writer puts it, this parable "calls forth all the resources of psychology." Indeed, Salvatore Garofalo has done us a great service by analyzing the behavior of the younger son. He writes:

From the very beginning, the striking thing about the story is the insolence of the younger son: *Father, give me the portion of the substance which falleth to me.* The cruelty and finality with which the younger son leaves his home are emphasised by a number of details:

not many days after—perhaps just long enough to find a buyer; *gathering all together went abroad into a far country*, which in Hebrew meant a land beyond the seas, thus opening an abyss, as it were, between father and son. The prodigal makes this clean break in order to see life; and there wasted his substance, living riotously. In other words, he wasted what his father had given him, for it was in fact a gift, not an inheritance; the prodigal made no effort to make his own personal fortune nor to show his own constructive ability, nor to use his new independence to develop a more forceful personality. He put as much distance as possible between himself and his father with the sole aim of escaping all advice and control.[3]

There is value in recalling these small details, given by Christ that we may preserve a right proportion between the malice and insolence of the boy in the story and the extreme triviality of many of the small sins which we confess. And when we come to the distinction between mortal sin and venial sin, we need to keep in mind the fate of this wastrel whose sin almost brought him to his death. Salvatore Garofalo brings this out excellently, when describing the prodigal in his distress.

This, then, is what sin is; a betrayal of a father's love and protection, the abuse of his gifts, abandoning home, the squandering of one's possessions, and the loss of one's dignity; humiliation, misery, hunger; the total destruction of a man, an existence worse than death itself.

Let us leave the boy here. You may side with those who maintain that in his misery he repented; I feel that he said no more than "It will pay me to go home." You may think that the speech which he rehearsed en route showed true contrition; I see it as no more than the best way of getting round the old man. Had he been able to find a new job or another patron, he would not have returned. There was nothing generous or gentle about this boy. What does it matter, for the parable concerns the father, who saw him a long way off, ran out to meet him, cut into his speech, gave immediate orders for a banquet, not because the son was sorry but from joy that something lost had been found. In our era of broken homes and generation gaps, such a situation is not uncommon; I know any number of parents who would have their child back at any price.

Every now and then, questions are put to me about humor in religion and why it is that, in the gospel, there are few jokes and no laughs. There are one or two who must have laughed, the Samaritan women, Matthew and the other publicans who sat down with Jesus for dinner, and the Best Man at Cana when the best wine was kept to the last. We know that the Eastern mind differs from ours and recall that, in the days before printing, all documents were handwritten; one can appreciate the unwillingness to waste precious effort on a few trivial Ha Ha's. But if laughter is restricted to Abraham and his wife—and theirs was cynical—we meet in the gospel a far more enduring happiness, namely, joy. Joy is one of the virtues most frequently recorded in the gospel, a point often overlooked.

The first mention of joy is found at the very start of St. Luke's gospel for, when Mary visited Elizabeth in the hill country, the babe in Elizabeth's womb jumped for joy. And when the baby was born, all her friends and neighbors, hearing of the Lord's kindness, "hurried round to share her joy." To the frightened shepherds at Bethlehem the angel gave this message: "Do not be afraid, listen, I bring you tidings of great joy, a joy to be shared by the whole people. Today, in the town of David, a saviour has been born to you; he is Christ, the Lord."

Christ himself often spoke about joy, as in that lovely passage: "A woman in childbirth suffers because her time has come, but when she has given birth to the child she forgets the suffering in her joy that a man has been born into the world." In the very same homily at the last supper, Christ promises to share with us his joy: "But now I am coming to thee; and while I am still in the world, I am telling them this so that my joy may be theirs and reach its full measure in them."

A striking fact which should never be forgotten is that Christ speaks most often of joy when he is dealing with the forgiveness of sin. So in these three parables about sin, the atmosphere is joyous and the shepherd who has found his sheep invites his neighbors to come and rejoice with him. The housewife who recovered her silver piece probably spent double the amount on light refreshments. "Rejoice with me," said she to her neighbors, "I have found the coin that was lost." At the end of this second parable, Christ made a baffling statement: "I tell you this, there will be more rejoicing in heaven over one repentant sinner than over ninety-nine virtuous men who have no need for repentance."

I used to think that such a statement was a little unfair. I used to wonder why the shepherd would risk his flock to chase after one maverick. Mine was the mentality of the elder brother of the prodigal when he heard the sound of music and dancing as he trudged home after a hard day in the fields. Was Christ suggesting that it was better to be a sinner, that God preferred sinners to the just who kept away from sin? The father of the prodigal gave the answer when he went outside to pacify the indignant boy. He never said that he loved the prodigal more; he never condoned his sin or spoke about forgiveness. All that he could say was that he, as a father, could not suppress or contain his joy: "It was only right we should celebrate and rejoice because your brother here was dead and has come to life; he was lost and is found."

Joy, then, is the word most often used in the gospel to describe God's reaction to one who repents. To judge by St. Augustine's approach, the sacrament of penance, as we now call it, should be the happiest of the sacraments. All too often it is not. Had our ancestors only named it the sacrament of forgiveness, we might have been spared some of its gloomier overtones. The funereal faces in the confessional queue bring back the memory of schooldays and the long wait outside the headmaster's room. Or to watch the struggle, sometimes lasting for several years, before a man can bring himself to go to confession is to suspect that many Christians have in mind a different type of father from the one who welcomed the prodigal home.

Has this lack of joy in the sacrament come from the Church, from individual priests, from teaching in school, from an alien, puritan background which has so gravely affected Christians in the English-speaking world? No doubt we are all partly to blame—penitents, clergy, teachers—that the gospel joy of forgiveness has been obscured. Confessionals are dingy, penitents look resentful, priests appear bored. Compare the exhilaration of Augustine, the exuberance of G.K.C. when it came to forgiveness, with the true but depressing description of his first confession given by such a sincere and spiritual writer as Graham Greene. Greene made his first confession when he was received into the Church in Nottingham in 1926:

The first General Confession which precedes conditional baptism and which covers the whole of a man's previous life is a humiliating ordeal. Later we may become hardened to the formulas of confession and sceptical about ourselves; we may only half intend to keep the promises we make until continual failure or the circumstances of our private life finally make it impossible to make any promises at all and many of us abandon confession and communion and join the foreign legion of the Church and fight for a city of which we are no longer full citizens. But in the first confession, a convert really believes in his own promises. I carried mine down with me like heavy stones into an empty corner of the Cathedral, dark already in the early afternoon, and the only witness to my baptism was a woman dusting chairs. I took the name Thomas, after St. Thomas the doubter, and not Thomas Aquinas, and then I went on to the Nottingham *Journal* office and the football results and the evening of potato chips. I remember very clearly the nature of my emotion as I walked away from the Cathedral; there was no joy in it at all.[4]

How sad the transition from the joy of that father, slaying the fattened calf, to Nottingham Cathedral, "dark already in the early afternoon." Chesterton became a Catholic in 1922 "because of the Church's practical power of dealing with sin." Chesterton was joyful and he made his first confession "in a kind of shed with a corrugated iron roof and wooden walls—part of the Railway Hotel, for at that time Beaconsfield had no Catholic church." Four years later Graham Greene, equally sincere, no less earnest, underwent the same experience and walked away with "no joy in it at all."

With the father of the prodigal in mind together with Christ's constant emphasis on joy and rejoicing, one becomes aware that something in our modern rit-

ual of penance is wrong. If this is borne out in Graham
Greene's sad account, it is further underlined in the behavior of those scrupulous people for whom confession
is an agonizing exercise. One good thing may be said
about the prodigal, he was not scrupulous. With such
a father, he did not need to be. Yet in certain periods
of Church history scruples were very much in fashion,
and a tender or delicate conscience was much prized.
Scruples normally pertain to the second dimension and
are a certain symptom of the divided self. They are not
basically religious and one meets innumerable scrupulous people with no beliefs of any kind. One poor soul,
whom I met recently, would test the lock on the back
door six or seven times a night.

No one has better described the convulsions of a
religiously scrupulous person than Sir Thomas More.
Sitting in his cell in the Tower of London, awaiting ex-
ecution, the Man for All Seasons wrote one of the best
accounts that I have read. This passage should restore
our joy in forgiveness by giving us a chance, if we are
scrupulous, to laugh at ourselves. The man who wrote
it had death just around the corner and that final moment when he would put all his trust in God.

> Thus fares the scrupulous person who frames for him-
> self more than double the fear that he needs and many
> times a greater fear when there is no cause for fear at
> all. Of that which is no sin at all, he makes a venial sin;
> that which is venial, he imagines to be mortal, and yet,
> for all this, continues to fall into them because of their
> very nature they are things that no man can live long
> without.
>
> Next, he fears that he is not fully and properly
> confessed, nor never fully contrite and, then, that his
> sins will never be forgiven him; so, then, he confesses
> and confesses again to the burden both of himself and

of his confessor. Then, every prayer that he recites, though he said it as well as the frail infirmity of man will suffer, yet he is not satisfied unless he says it again and, after that, again. And when he has said one thing thrice, he is as little satisfied with the last as with the first and, then, his heart is forever heavy and restless and in fear, full of doubt and dullness without comfort or spiritual repose. With this fear of the night, the devil sorely troubles the mind of many a right good man and reduces him to some great inconvenience. For he will drive him if he can so much to think of the rigours of God's justice that he will keep him from pondering on the comfortable remembrance of God's great mighty mercy and so make him do all his good works wearily.[5]

A great many holy people are troubled by scruples for a time. Even saints as balanced as St. Teresa of Ávila, St. Ignatius of Loyola, and St. Francis de Sales were plagued with anxieties and scruples in the first stages of their spiritual advance. The depression vanished for good when they came to know Christ more intimately and worried less about themselves.

Let Augustine end this chapter for he, perhaps, more than any other saint, came to confession through joy. Yet he on his own admission and for many years had been a deliberate sinner, had no doubts about his past transgressions; his need for forgiveness in the present moment was a red-hot reality. His *Confessions* are a nonstop dialogue with God. He saw that forgiveness requires such a dialogue between two persons in the third dimension, heart to heart. Dare we presume such an intimate relationship with God?

Augustine had doubts at first at a moment of great sadness when an intimate friend died:

That huge load of misery which was first to be lightened and afterwards removed by thee, O Lord, lay heavy upon me. I knew it but I would not, or could not, seek the remedy because when I thought of thee, it was not anything substantial or firm that came into my mind; nor was it thou but my own vain imagination and error which was, indeed, my God at that time. Whither was it possible for my heart to fly from my heart? Whither could I escape from myself?[6]

In the end, a sudden appreciation of Christ's three parables changed Augustine's attitude to sin. He asks God what there is in man that gives God more joy in forgiving a sinner than in dealing with the just who need no forgiveness and, next, almost as though he had heard the answer, he exclaims: "We listen with joy whenever we are told of the lost sheep carried home on the shoulder of the shepherd, rejoicing; and when the coin is restored to thy treasury, her neighbors rejoicing with the poor woman who found it."

It is Augustine's theory that joy has no meaning without sorrow, that the greater the pain before it, the greater the joy. Thus sailors rejoice when a storm is over and men best enjoy food who were hungry before.

A friend is sick and his pulse threatens danger; all who long for his recovery are sick in mind with him. He is restored though he walks not with his former strength; yet there is such joy as was not present before, when he walked sound and strong. Of the return of the prodigal, he says to God with so much feeling, "The joy of the house brings tears to our eyes."

6—A LESSON FROM
LITTLEMORE

An obvious temptation faces any author, the urge to arrange things neatly under points one, two, and three. By such a device he may gain precision, but life itself is rarely so orderly. Writing about confession, my thoughts may be tidy; inside the box, if I ever get there, I am speechless, muddled, and in tears.

As already pointed out, the psychologists like to arrange their findings under headings one, two, and three. Thus their analysis of man reveals him simultaneously in three dimensions, identified by Dr. Frankl as the physical, mental, and spiritual. Writing about human motivation, the same author gives us the will-to-pleasure, the will-to-power, and the will-to-meaning; another neat arrangement inside a triangular frame. From other psychologists we are offered three levels, three ways of life, three tapes, three recordings, and, who knows in the not too distant future, three blind mice.

The same mystic number three turns up in theology whenever the sacrament of penance is discussed. As children we knew that contrition, confession, and satisfaction were required and in the old "Confiteor" we dutifully struck our breast three times and admitted that we had sinned exceedingly in thought, word, and deed. As likely as not, the priest would then say, "For your penance say three Hail Marys," to which one timid child answered, "Father, I only know one."

Some people place great store on mystic numbers,

St. Augustine one. Years ago, I remember rubbing my eyes in South Chicago when a rabbi, recovering from surgery, attributed his cure to the numbers on his theater trolley which matched some mystical figures supplied by the prophet Daniel. Who knows? Points one, two, and three are somehow all linked to our three dimensions and show how important these may be. One day, when we join St. Paul in the third heaven, we may discover how our three dimensions derive from the three persons of the Trinity.

After laughing at such a neat arrangement, let me offer you a final one, two, three. This last triplet proves of great practical value when considering the subject of sin. For sin may be approached from three angles, and we have a legal, a theological, and a psychological view of sin. Any muddle in our minds between these may produce great sorrow and anxiety. This I have seen in many questions about confession that have been put to me. These questions stem from a basic query, expressed by different people differently. One questioner put it neatly: "What I say in confession is not what is wrong with me." Another will word it: "I don't feel sorry; I cannot believe that God would take my list of peccadilloes seriously." Those of delicate conscience blame themselves: "I must be a hypocrite; I seem unable to examine my conscience properly." Statements such as these suggest some confusion between the legal, theological, and psychological views of sin.

In our present transitional age, with attitudes swiftly changing, a further worry appears. Those who ask questions about confession often add a postscript: "I used to go to confession often but now I seem to be falling away." To the distaste of going to confession is added a sense of guilt for not having been. Yet the frequency of going to confession may be viewed legally, theologically, and psychologically. A sinner who sincerely tries to fulfill the legal or theological requirements may psychologically be confessing far too frequently. These and other worries may be discussed in later chapters but here let us give our attention to contrition, the basic quality needed for the forgiveness of sin. One must think this out for oneself.

I found no better way of satisfying myself about these three approaches than that of studying the gospel scene. The world may have changed but sin remains the same.

(1) No one who reads the gospel can miss the legal view of sin. The scribes and Pharisees, not wholly to their discredit, knew, loved, studied, and defended the Mosaic law. Those who today clamor for an unstructured Church should remember that the rules and regulations imposed by Moses were revealed to him by God. Societies flourish in the first, physical, dimension and cannot survive without laws. The Pharisees were not wrong in recognizing this. On such issues as adultery, ritual washings, Sabbath day observance, they studied the traditions and issued guidelines so that the law might be understood. As with lawyers in any age, some used the law to line their own pockets, to feather their own nest. Christ denounced those who were hard on others and did not observe the law themselves. Both he and St. Paul respected the law; they found it wooden but this did not mean that it was wrong.

After the destruction of the temple and the sack of the holy city, exiled Pharisees fled to the township of Jamnia to resume their researches again. Josephus, apostate and Pharisee, who went to Rome and gained an impressive reputation, secretly admired his old-time colleagues and their brave persistency.

In the Church of today we, too, have our lawyers

and moralists. As Newman wrote, "We are guided in our ordinary duties by the books of moral theology which are drawn up by theologians of authority and experience as an instruction to our confessors . . . Reducible as these directions, in detail, are to a few and simple heads which I have mentioned, they are little more than reflections and memoranda of our moral sense, unlike the positive enactments of the Legislature."[1] How many of those lists of sins which we were taught as children derived from this good but academic source.

(2) While the scribes and Pharisees continued to debate how many fresh eggs a man could carry on the Sabbath, Christ and St. Paul were unfolding to the world a vast and impressive theology of sin. Why, John the Baptist was preaching forgiveness before Christ had said a word. To identify himself with sinners, Christ stood in the queue to be baptized. From then until his death, forgiveness of sin was to be for him a central subject, the very heart of the liturgy of the last supper from which all Christian liturgies derive. Two thousand years later, at Mass every morning, I say, "This is the chalice of my blood, the blood of the new and everlasting covenant, which will be shed for you and for all men so that sins may be forgiven." Calvary, the sacraments, the Mass, the very concept of sacrifice, from the days of Abraham down to the great epistle to the Hebrews, derive their meaning and purpose from the theology of sin.

(3) A third approach to sin in the gospel story was hinted at earlier in this book. The psychology of each sinner, in that strange, obscure world of the third dimension, proves all-important where sorrow and forgiveness are involved. Let that prostitute who entered the Pharisee's house while Christ was at table represent

every other sinner who has been drawn towards him. She was sobbing but not because she had broken the law of Moses in any legal sense. Had this been the worry, she could have consulted the Pharisee, presiding at the dinner, for he could have rattled off the regulations for her defilement to be erased. But, as we read in the epistle to the Hebrews, such rules were insufficient, they could not "bring any worshipper to perfection in his inner self; they are rules about the outward life." She stood there weeping; her needs were far deeper than that. She was not interested in the legal view of sin nor was it an interest in theology that brought her sobbing and uninvited to this hostile dining room.

At the center of her heart—we may judge this by our own—was an awareness of her weakness, misery, and failure and, behind such pain, a relief that she had met someone so understanding that she could be herself and give herself away. In her profession, she hired out her first dimension but her heart needed more than cash. Behind all the misery and squalor of every type of sin remains a grain of hope. Christ kindled and revivified such flickering hopes.

It helps me greatly to analyze such gospel situations as this. I note that she said nothing, confessed nothing but revealed everything. She had no need to recite any act of contrition, for her tears were more eloquent than words. In plain words, she did no more than summon up sufficient courage to do something about her desolate situation, to run down the street, gate-crash a door, run weeping into a righteous dining room. Her tears were her acts of contrition. Francis de Sales in a conference went even further. He remarked, "A sigh may be enough."

She never saw or guessed Christ's view of the picture, seated as he was as the guest of honor in a righteous and hypocritical home. He saw her tears and felt the disapproval; he said to his host, "Much has been forgiven her because she has loved much." In this bewildering situation, of first-dimensional impersonations, only Christ and a common prostitute spoke heart to heart.

When Christ said, "I am the Way and the Truth and the Life," he covered all three dimensions, showing us the way to behave in the physical world around us, the truth for our mental dimension and a new and fuller life in the heart. That frightened, unwanted girl, who sobbed but said nothing, yearned for this fuller life and little more. The Pharisee watched the scene with scorn from the center of the high table, wondering how a human being could bring herself so low. But, as Newman wrote of sinners, "They rise by falling. Plainly so, for no condescension can be as great as that of Our Lord himself. The more they debase themselves, the more they are like to him, and the more they are like to him, the greater must be their power with him."

No need here to repeat the whole story; enough that Christ turned to the scornful man beside him. "Simon," he said, "I have something to say to you."

This scene long baffled me. I thought I knew everything about contrition, having practiced it and preached on it for years. I knew, for example, that sorrow must be in the present moment or not at all. We may be sorry for the past but our act of sorrow must be a spontaneous reaction, in the third dimension, at the red-hot point of consciousness. That girl was sorry in the present moment; Christ saw her weeping now. I knew that, though memory is a precious gift—a man who loses it becomes half a cabbage—it cannot be trusted to give me an exact picture of the past. In retreats, I have often urged men and women to be sorry in the present and not to worry unduly about the details of past sins. Motives cannot be reconstructed or reweighed. There are acts which if done today would be gravely sinful but which looked harmless thirty years ago. I know now that the same could be stated the other way round. I have known for years the feeling that my friend expressed so neatly, "What I say in confession is not what is wrong with me."

Many times in conferences and retreats, I have made the point that confession is very much easier for someone who has committed a grave sin. Were I to strike a Papal legate, I would have no problem about what to say. But bad temper, sulking, name-dropping, scrounging sound so trivial and hardly seem to justify the fuss. Yet, thanks to an unusual word by Cardinal Newman, the counting up of small sins now makes sense. Newman was describing the way in which the thoughts and ideas of individuals are absorbed by society as a whole. He writes of them being percolated, a word familiar to all of us who like our coffee fresh. "Doctrine, too," says Newman, "is percolated, as it were through different minds."[2] The description helps me greatly for, even with each individual, a kind of percolation is perceptible. Take the case of that weeping girl; she probably knew nothing of theology and yet, in her heart, had absorbed the story of Adam in a strained, filtered, or vaporized form. In our own case, the legal approach to sin and the theological view of sin are not recognizable in the third dimension but, in a percolated form, they play their part.

The image of the percolator helps us to make sense, an unpleasant sense, of our trivial, weekly sins. They do not add up to much, they cannot be recalled or identified, but the resultant cup of coffee in the third dimension leaves a very bitter taste in the heart.

I think I learned more about sin from Newman than from any other source. For Newman directs our attention not so much to sin as to God. He accepts the role of the priest as judge and adviser but insists in the spirit of King David that we confess our sins primarily to God. "For I am well aware of my faults, I have my sin constantly before my mind, having sinned against none other than you, having done what you regard as wrong." Such an attitude, basic to confession, is, I think, threatened in the modern Church. We have come to regard confession as a burden, imposed by the Church. For some it is no more than a liturgical ritual or a counseling session which is sometimes helpful but more often not. Among some, there is the view that sin is not an individual but a community weakness and that we sin chiefly against our fellow men.

Newman pulls us up with a start. He pens, I suggest, a picture of that Pharisee who scorned the poor sinner and, reading it, I came to realize how closely it resembled me:

We find these men possessed of many virtues, but proud, bashful, fastidious and reserved. Why is this? It it is because they think and act as if there was nothing really objective in their religion; it is because conscience for them is not the word of a lawgiver, as it ought to be, but the dictate of their own minds and nothing more; it is because they do not look out of themselves, because they do not look through and beyond their own minds to their Maker but are engrossed in notions of what is due to themselves, their own dignity and their own consistency. Their conscience has become a mere self-respect . . . When they do wrong, they feel, not contrition of which God is the object, but remorse and a

sense of degradation. They call themselves fools, not
sinners; they are angry and impatient, but not humble.
They shut themselves up in themselves; it is a misery to
them to think or speak of their own feelings; it is a
misery to suppose that others see them and their
shyness, and their sensitiveness often becomes morbid.
As to confession, which is so natural to the Catholic, to
them it is impossible; unless, in cases where they have
been guilty, an apology is due to their own character; is
expected of them and will be satisfactory to look back
upon. They are victims of an intense self-contempla-
tion.[3]

"Simon," said Christ, "I have something to say to
you."

Once one starts quoting Newman, it is difficult to
find any good reason to stop. I risk one further quotation for if, in the passage just quoted, Newman hits off
Simon and myself, in another vivid paragraph he draws
the high-class, academic outlines of that weeping girl:

Who can deny the existence of conscience? Who does
not feel the force of its injunctions? But how dim is the
illumination in which it is invested and how feeble its
influence compared with that evidence of sight and
touch which is the foundation of Physical Science. How
easily can we be talked out of our clearest views of duty.
How does this or that moral precept crumble into nothing when we rudely handle it; how does the fear of sin
pass off from us, as quickly as the glow of modesty dies
away from the countenance, and we say, "It is all superstition." However, after a time, we look round and then,
to our surprise, we see as before the same law of duty,
the same moral precepts, the same protests against sin,
appearing over against us, in their old places, as if they
never had been brushed away, like the divine hand-
writing upon the wall at the banquet.[4]

And Jesus said to Simon, "I tell you, her sins, which are many, are forgiven for she loved much."

Recently I revisited Littlemore, Newman's retreat outside Oxford from 1842 to 1845. When I was an undergraduate at Oxford, nearly forty years ago, Littlemore was unbearable, a village shattered by the heavy traffic on the main London road. The traffic has now been diverted, the buildings restored, and a group of devoted people tend the garden and show one to Newman's room. I knelt in the same place as he had knelt, more than a century ago.

The saintly Italian priest who had spent five hours in the rain on the top of a coach to get to Littlemore, described the scene thus: "I took up my position by the fire to dry myself; the door opened—and what a spectacle it was for me to see at my feet John Henry Newman, begging me to hear his confession and to admit him into the bosom of the Catholic Church. And there, by the fire, he began his general confession with extraordinary humility and devotion." A note tells us that Newman finished his first confession next day.[5]

Newman, we know, to prepare for the great moment, had stayed indoors all day. He writes later, to a friend, "The moment before acting may be, as can easily be imagined, peculiarly dreary—the mind may be confused—no reason for acting may be forthcoming . . . I could do nothing but shut myself up in my room and lie down on my bed."

I knelt by the fireplace in Newman's room at Littlemore and read a thought of his, printed on a pious card: "Faith is founded on the knowledge that God is almighty; Hope is founded on the knowledge that God is all-merciful."

7—THE WHY-THERAPY

Even submarines have to surface and we, certainly, cannot remain in the thrilling world of the third dimension for long. Mystics and contemplatives apart, most human beings are able to endure the solitude and nakedness for only a few minutes, in the manner of those trying their first sauna bath. Christ told us "it is from the overflow of the heart that the mouth speaks." The heart is designed to overflow like a fountain and, sooner or later, we are deposited in the second dimension with our hearts in our mouths.

In this book, we have spent many chapters underground in the third dimension because any true understanding of the gospel demands familiarity in this field. Without it, our view of Christ would be superficial and our welcome no warmer than the one he met in that Pharisee's house. But if one may study the workings of the heart without exhaustion, direct personal experience of our innermost being has to be limited. Few of us have the strength sufficient to isolate the heart and to cut it off from thought and action for long. The length of time varies very much with different people and even in the same person from day to day. Time is useless in the third dimension; the bottom of the heart is timeless so one need not attempt to measure acts of sorrow by the clock. A true act of contrition may be over in a flash.

Back in the second dimension, we are inclined to divide our prayers into neat sections as though filling sandwiches with him. The prayer books give us acts of faith, hope, charity, contrition to be devoured one at a time. In the third dimension I find that these operations fuse into one. Augustine wrote, "The act of adoration of a sinner is an act of contrition," a view that helped me much. Years ago, I found this in the prayer of Manasses: "I bow down the knee of my heart and I adore thee"; it takes but a second to genuflect at the red-hot point of consciousness.

Conflicting attitudes to confession confront us at this point. Where the Church sees man as a whole and counts in all three dimensions, there are those who limit confession to the third dimension and like to confess their sins only to God. Luther was one of these. "To feel," "to experience" are favorite expressions of his. His basic dogma, justification by faith alone, is directly traceable to his own experience in the confessional. As one author puts it, "Seeking assurance of forgiveness, he claims to have found it neither in his own acts of repentance nor in the objective efficacy of the priest's absolution but in the acceptance by faith of God's promise to forgive." Both Luther and Calvin retain confession as a sacrament, see the seemliness of going to a minister, allow for penitential services in church. Luther adds, "Secret confession as practiced now, though unprovable from Scripture, is highly commendable, useful, even necessary." Yet the absolution of a priest achieved nothing and the contrition and confession of the penitent was unnecessary. Faith in God's promise of forgiveness is very much a third-dimensional experience.

William James, writing more than three centuries after Luther, comments on this doctrine and its sad, unexpected consequence:

The complete decay of the practice of confession in Anglo-Saxon communities is a little hard to account for.

Reaction against popery is, of course, the historic expla-
nation, for in popery, confession went with penances
and absolution and other inadmissible practices. But on
the side of the sinner himself, it seems as if the need
ought to have been too great to accept so summary a
refusal of its satisfaction. One would think that in
more men the shell of secrecy would have had to open,
the pent-in abscess to burst and gain relief, even though
the ears that heard the confession were unworthy. The
Catholic Church, for obvious utilitarian reasons, has sub-
stituted auricular confession to one priest for the more
radical act of public confession. We English-speaking
Protestants, in the general self-reliance and unsociability
of our nature, seem to find it enough if we take God
alone into our confidence.[1]

Is it enough for the balance and happiness of the
whole man to take God alone into our confidence?
Much earlier in this book, I quoted the view of Dr.
Paul Tournier, the devout Swiss Calvinist: "There are
all around us vast numbers of people who are sick for
confession." These need to take two into their
confidence, God and their psychiatrist.

Luther found no assurance of forgiveness in the priest's
absolution where Thomas More, Chesterton, Newman,
and how many thousands of others reacted the other
way round. This was brought home to me by my own
father, who, in his early twenties, was received into the
Catholic Church. At the time he was an Anglican on
paper and, as I presume, who knew him later, full of
deep thoughts. As a boy of seventeen, he volunteered
and served with the Highland Light Infantry in the
Boer War. A man of peace, he was to spend another
four years in the trenches in World War One. He used
to remind me when I was young that we cradle Catho-

lics took confession very much for granted, having lived with it all our lives. He had not. He would describe how he would kneel by his bed at night to express some kind of sorrow, never knowing for certain whether God had forgiven him or not. Over the years, there accumulated for him what he described as a spiritual dunghill about which he could do no more than pray and keep his fingers crossed. Once inside the Church, confession for him not only lit up God's mercy but a special act of mercy, through which God permitted a man, a priest, to make a visible gesture, an outward sign of inward peace.

This is not the place to restart the battle of the texts. At the Reformation, protagonists hurled chunks of Scripture at each other with few obvious results. Reading back, it becomes clear that issue was joined on contemporary practices and abuses, not on the basic doctrine of the forgiveness of sin. Protestants and Catholics alike knew that forgiveness was essential to the gospel, that Christ forgave sins himself, on two solemn occasions passed on his power to others, which powers were used by the twelve in the very early Church. Let one example suffice here; we read in the Acts of the Apostles about the Christians at Ephesus: "Many believers came forward, confessing their evil practices and giving a full account of them; and a number of those who followed magic arts made their books into a heap and burned them in public; the value of these was reckoned up and proved to be fifty thousand silver pieces." No one would wish to argue that this incident was identical with confession as we know it today. Much more important is the fact that the Church had a practical power of dealing with sin from the very beginning and this through the agency of men. I find it moving that Luther, Calvin, and the

Roman apologists, while abusing one another, had at heart the Christian spirit of mercy and the common desire to make forgiveness as easy as possible for men. Each saw in the other's point of view an imposition and a burden which Christ would never have instituted and which he would have wanted to remove. Abuses, alas, are always possible where men are concerned. But far deeper than these is the desire in man to express his sorrow in all three dimensions and to enjoy the certainty of forgiveness conveyed visibly to sinners in Christ's day.

Thousands of technical tomes must have been written about confession across the centuries. Happily I need not examine them here or quote them, for the Catholic sense of the sacrament of penance has been set out simply by St. Francis de Sales. How frequently in my lifetime has this great saint and doctor solaced me. Here, in his eighteenth Spiritual Conference he says:

Before learning how we ought to prepare ourselves to receive the Sacraments and what fruit we ought to derive from their reception, we must first understand what Sacraments are and what their effects are. The Sacraments then are channels, through which, so to speak, God descends to us as we through prayer ascend to him, since prayer is nothing else than the lifting up of the mind and heart to God. The effects of the Sacraments are various although they all have but one and the same aim and object which is to unite us to God. By the Sacrament of Baptism, we unite ourselves to God as a son to his father; by that of Confirmation as a soldier to his captain, getting strength to fight and to conquer our enemies and temptations; by the Sacrament of Penance we are united to God like reconciled friends. Now, these are the different effects of the Sacraments but they all demand the union with God.[2]

This description pleases me for it underlines the union between myself and God. Next, the outward sign in the sacrament is not some type of magic but God's share in a dialogue. There can be no doubt that God is able to forgive us our sins without confession; the need for an outward sign is on our side, not on his. Thirdly, could there be a better title than the sacrament of reconciled friends?

Writers as sensitive as de Sales and Newman approach confession in a spirit which is less and less common today. Ours is a penal approach, a schoolboy attitude, that we have been caught, we must confess because the Church so tells us; it is easier to get it over and take our punishment. Were we, for a moment, to recall the joy of the gospels, we would appreciate far better the reunion of reconciled friends. Newman retained this joy and liked to quote the words of his dear friend Keble: "Friends do not ask for literal commands; from their knowledge of the speaker, they understand his half-words and from love of him they anticipate his wishes." Francis de Sales, stressing the right intention needed for confession, returns to the desire of union with God and to "rendering ourselves more pleasing to him, without any admixture of private interest." The sacrament of reconciliation should mean much more than rattling off a shopping list of small offenses; it is the sacrament for those who know their own weakness and who do not believe in themselves.

As the question of what to confess proves an enduring problem to many people, we should, perhaps, consider it here. We may ask St. Francis first and his immediate answer is rich in common sense:

I would not have you so scrupulous and anxious about confessing numbers of trifling imperfections, since we are not even obliged to confess venial sins if we do not wish to. If however we do confess them, we must firmly resolve to amend, otherwise it would be an abuse of confession. Nor must we torment ourselves when we cannot remember our faults so as to confess them, for it is incredible that a soul who frequently examines herself should not have noticed sufficiently any faults of importance as to remember them. As regards these many but trifling defects, you may speak to the Lord about them whenever you perceive them; an act of self-humiliation, a sigh, will be enough for that.

If you were God, what kind of confessions would you be pleased to hear? Such a question is not blasphemous for, if you recall, Christ began his three parables of forgiveness by asking the people, "Which one among you would not feel the same?" Surely the point of the incarnation is that Christ as a man saw things in our way. Which mother among us does not know joy and satisfaction when a toddler says sorry spontaneously and in a sincere way? Which wife has not felt "if only he had told me openly"? In every human relationship there are grades of reconciliation and an ascending order of sympathy. I hardly have to eavesdrop in our supermarket to hear the old gossips writing this paragraph for me. Such clichés as "No, dear, I can feel no sympathy for him"; "Well, she brought it on herself but I must say that she is making an effort"; "If you knew what I know about them, you'd make allowances"; "Yes, I know he talks big but he does not really mean it," provide an accurate guide to Christ's way of thought. There was no character in the gospel whom Christ did not want to forgive. Yet he felt no sympathy at all with that servant who, forgiven a large debt, prosecuted another for a debt which was small. He showed small sympathy for Herod, much sympathy for Pilate, loved Martha without heeding her grumbling because Mary was not helping with the work. What Christ wants in confession is what he wanted also in the gospel, the sincere and contrite heart.

A priest sitting in the confessional, as I have done over thirty years for heaven knows how many thousands of hours, comes to see the sacrament from Christ's point of view. He knows very well that all who enter the confessional, himself included, want to be sincere. He comes to appreciate this portmanteau sacrament designed to cover worries of any size. Newman took two days over his first confession, and St. Ignatius of Loyola records in his autobiography, "When he came to Montserrat, after much prayer, he made a written general confession of his sins with the confessor's consent and spread it over three days."[3] Readers may think that such would not happen in our day and how wrong they would be. At certain, unexpected moments in life, often in times of sorrow, failure, fear, or crisis, a person is drawn to face reality. Alcoholics Anonymous knows this well. One of the most touching moments in my priestly life came with a young man of twenty-four, not a Catholic, who wished to join the AA or a similar organization. He had been asked to fill in a survey of his life, find a minister of religion and go through it with him. The interview took three hours. When he had gone, I found myself trembling with shame and confusion, never having attained to such sincerity as this.

If the sacrament is designed to cover cases of this kind, it is also suited to the needs of good, untroubled people, to Martha, Mary, and Lazarus. These have little to say but yearn to make the gesture; their sorrow is in their feet as they enter the box. Some, of course, come to confession, as they also went to Christ, for less worthy motives, self-pity and resentment; in a roundabout way, they confess not their own sins but the wrongs that others have done to them. Such cases are rare. Over the years, I have watched simple, quiet people attain to great holiness through the strength which this sacrament provides.

One lesson I have learned as a confessor from my experience as a penitent: never shrug off or belittle the small faults which people choose to confess. Should a confessor say, "There is nothing in that," or "Don't bother to confess this," the heart of the penitent sinks. On one memorable occasion, I confessed a small sin and the priest said, "I'm glad you confessed that; it is worth watching," and I left the box unexplainably happy and refreshed.

Some complain dolefully, "What's the use, Father? I say the same old things week after week." To which I would like to answer, "Aren't you lucky; wouldn't it be slightly awkward if you had a brand-new line every time?" The plain fact is that the choleric, the sanguine, and the melancholy stand a very good chance of confessing the same sins all their lives. There are, too, sins which those of a certain temperament will never have to confess. I could never confess that I have been lazy; it is precisely this not-being-lazy that is wrong with me.

I am determined to introduce an old friend, Theodore Parker, at this point. I came upon him in 1946 in William James's *The Varieties of Religious Experience.* He interested me so much that I pieced together biographical scraps about him, culled chiefly from *Chamber's Encyclopaedia* of 1901. More than a century ago, Theodore was saying to the people of Boston what many, myself at one time included, are thinking today. Theodore Parker was a distinguished Unitarian minister, a graduate of Harvard, who worked in the

Roxbury area of Boston in 1836. In the War of Independence, his grandfather had held a command at Lexington. Theodore, we are told, drew three thousand people weekly to his sermons at Melodeon Hall and at the Boston Music Hall. Sadly enough, this great revivalist developed consumption; a lecture tour in Europe failed to help him and he died in Florence in 1860 when he was just fifty years old.

The thousands who packed Melodeon Hall of a Sunday evening went home happy and encouraged by such eloquence as this:

> Orthodox scholars say that, in the heathen classics, you find no consciousness of sin. It is very true—thank God for it. They were conscious of wrath, of cruelty, avarice, drunkenness, lust, sloth, cowardice and other actual vices and struggled to get rid of these deformities: but they were not conscious of "Enmity against God" and did not sit down and whine and groan against nonexistent evil. I have done wrong things enough in my life and do them now; I miss the mark, draw the bow and try again. But I am not conscious of hating God or man or right or love and I know there is much health in me; and in my body even now there dwelleth many a good thing in spite of consumption and St. Paul.[1]

The robust common sense of Theodore Parker encouraged me greatly, many years ago. If parents suffer for a child who runs itself down, lacks confidence, and courts failure, so, surely, God derives small pleasure from mock humility. Here is the mentality of Uriah Heap, of that craven steward in the gospel who from fear of failure buried his talent in the ground. Not a few people feel it necessary to exaggerate their uselessness and sinfulness. Theodore was not one of these, nor was St. Paul, who gladly admitted that he had fought a good fight and done pretty well. To overdo our sinfulness, to see failures everywhere will rob us of the joy of a reconciled friend.

Many years ago, in Belgium, lived a very holy priest with a high reputation for sanctity, named Père Petit. By chance two other priests with the same surname lived in the same community. One evening, the porter came to the common room to announce that Père Petit was wanted in the parlor and the superior asked, "Which Père Petit?" "The holy Père Petit," said the porter, at which the holy man stood up and said, "That's me."

Theodore Parker was right to find much good in himself but we must hope that he avoided the other pitfall for, if he believed in himself, he would have repeated Adam's mistake. Indeed, he would almost be back in the temple with that Pharisee who thanked God that he was not as other men. St. Paul, who loved to boast of all that he had suffered, knew very well the source of true humility. As he told the Corinthians: "We are the earthenware jars that hold this treasure, to make clear that such an overwhelming power comes from God and not from us."

Our utter dependence on God's grace is often forgotten by those who believe in themselves. Our confessions would seem less trivial if we assumed a more positive attitude. We do not confess because we are rotten but because we are weak. In many a gospel scene, the sinner needed encouragement as much as forgiveness and all went home refreshed. Those who say, "I do not go to confession; it does not do me any good," are talking through their hats. The saints confessed frequently and doffed their hats.

With one more comment on his cheery outlook, we may leave Theodore Parker for good. When he remarks, "I am not conscious of hating God," I would like to ask him, "Whoever is?" Over the years, I have never met anyone who was conscious of "hating God or man or right or love." The answer to Theodore Parker and to those with him lies in the legal, theological, and psychological views of sin. We have met these before. The legal attitude to sin as a breach of the law, grave or trivial, is covered by the canon lawyers and moralists. Next, we see sin in a theological sense, an offense against God first committed by Adam and repeated by every sinner since. In the theology of sin we see Christ die on Calvary. The catechism, quoting St. Paul, says, "Our Saviour died for our sins and those who sin grievously 'crucify again to themselves the Son of God, making him a mockery.'" In such a theological setting, it might possibly make sense to say that a grave sinner may be conscious of deliberately rejecting God.

Finally, we have the psychological approach to sin and in this lies the answer, for here we are conscious of choosing ourselves in place of God. This aspect the gospel teaches well. When Christ died on Calvary few if any of the perpetrators were conscious of hating God or even of hating Christ himself. Even the chief priests only wanted him out of the way to safeguard their establishment. When Caiaphas remarked, "It is expedient that one man should die of the people," he gave us the perfect word on which our examination of conscience should be based. Judas never hated Christ or God but he wanted money; Peter loved his master but his own safety more. Pilate did no more than wash his hands of the whole business, passing the buck to Herod, who only wanted fun. John Mark—if that was he—simply decided that it was safer not to go back to get his garments; he fled naked down the street.

In a sense, these were all trivial sins with no hatred

in them, sins which we ourselves commit by day. Had the sacrament of penance been in existence, Peter, in the three years before that cowardly denial, would have been scratching his head outside the box and wondering what on earth he could say.

One man alone stopped thinking of his own interests on that grim evening; with incredible bravery Judas went back to the priests, admitted his sin in public and threw the tainted money to the ground. Then, sadly enough, in panic, forgetting the three parables of forgiveness, he took his life.

I have called this chapter "The why-therapy" to preserve a most useful piece of advice. It was given to me by an old Marist Father in New Zealand; if I remember rightly, at the lovely town of Timaru. We were speaking about confession and he remarked that he had found it helpful, after a penitent had accused himself of something, to ask him why. I am unable to recall his exact words but the point of his theory was that many of us begin by confessing the wrong sins. When asked, "Why did you do this?" we shed our prepared formula and get down to the truth beneath. So, should a child confess, "I have been naughty," the New Zealand Marist would ask him why. Many kids used to be thrown into confusion because they were spouting a formula by rote. Every now and then a child would pinpoint the real fault and the situation. "Because I had to go to bed when we were playing a game." Here is an imaginary setting for a grain of truth.

Let me apply the "why-therapy" to a number of fictitious situations, all of which, I hope, mirror the realities of life. Thus one mother may confess, "I am very impatient with the children," and were I to ask her why, she would say, "Because they are so naughty," to which I would rejoin, "Such impatience with naughty children may well be more a virtue than a vice." A second mother says the same and if I ask her why, she answers, "I am impatient because I am so tired," and my "why" to this reaches halfway to the truthful answer; she says, "We go to bed too late at night." Were I brave enough to toss up another "why" I might get one or all of four honest answers: (a) TV (b) Bingo (c) Entertaining (d) My husband likes to go to the pub at night. And a "why" to these four might disclose whether she is treating the children fairly; whether she has committed a sin or not.

Outside confession and for the sake of this book I asked a friend to name his greatest worry and he replied immediately with scant reflection, "I love her but in recent years I have unending squabbles with my wife." Looking suitably holy, I lobbed up a little "why?" Said he, "I really don't know, Father. I suppose because she is always nagging at me." A third "Why?" produced a series of spluttered excuses, that his wife was a darling but overpious, a bit narrow-minded, something of a shrew. A fourth "why" was not required; of a sudden he sat up straight and remarked in the flat, formal tones of a TV announcer, "I drink too much."

In the gospels, the "why-therapy" is much in evidence. Judas asked, "Why should not this ointment have been sold for three hundred pence and given to the poor?" but St. John gave the true answer. "Now he said this not because he cared for the poor but because he was a thief." Were we to ask, "Why did the prodigal go home?" St. Luke tells us, "He came to himself and said, 'How many hired servants in my father's house abound with bread and here I perish with hunger?'" When the five foolish virgins arrived late at the wedding and banged on the door, they no doubt said, "We were delayed, we had to buy oil for our lamps." Had I been posted at that door, I would have asked them, "Why did you have to buy oil?"

The supreme example of the "why-therapy" begins in the gospel when Christ asks, "Why do you see the speck in your brother's eye and not the beam in your own?" Across the centuries, how very few have come anywhere near the true answer, given by Cardinal Newman; his "I see the speck in my brother's eye because I hate my brother" made me grasp how, unwittingly, dishonest I have been.

Sin which is divided into mortal and venial on the legal level in the first dimension, becomes the mockery of Christ on Calvary in the second dimension with which theology is concerned. As with coffee beans, the conclusions from these two dimensions percolate to the third. In the nebulous world of the third dimension all our "whys" are answered without words. Here we join in honest, open company with Pontius Pilate, Peter, Herod, Mary his mother, Judas, and the neighbors across the road. I long for the moment when I can ask Pilate, "Why did you wash your hands?" With Judas, who was so brave, the only "why" would be, "Why did you lose courage at the end?" I would ask Simon the Pharisee, "Why did you invite Christ to dinner in your house?" Zacheus, "Why did you climb that tree?" the Samaritan woman, "Why did you tell the whole village?" Mary his mother, "Why did you stand by the cross until the end?"

Herod the King would, in the third dimension, answer, "the will-to-pleasure," Pilate, Caiaphas, and many others would use that most honest and treacherous of words "expediency." Zacheus would, surely, admit that, as a short, middle-aged man, the climbing of a sycamore tree was in itself abhorrent but "the will-to-meaning" made the effort worthwhile. Mary his mother, faced with a "why," would have answered, "I love him" and here we reach the very peak of a human heart.

When I go to confession today, I examine my conscience with the aid of five words, all scriptural: "expediency," "cowardice," "pleasure," "power," "joy." Were you to see me in the confessional queue and to ask me, "Why are you going to confession?" I would have to answer, "I have seen the beam in my own eye."

8—THE WIND OF CHANGE

Though sanity, happiness, and peace are meaningful only in the present moment, few resist the temptation to live ahead. So today prophecies about life in the eighties are two-a-penny in newsprint and on the TV screens. We read about furniture for the eighties, socialism in the eighties, air travel through the eighties, with Big Brother due to arrive in 1984.

In contrast to this, the sacrament of penance in the nineteen eighties should remain very much as it is today. At heart and in the third dimension, human beings show little change. Our impersonations on the stage vary with current fashions but conscience does not alter and the causes of sin remain the same. Thousands of years ago, the same will-to-power that we know led Cain to kill his brother, and the will-to-pleasure persuaded David to interrupt his psalm writing to commit murder and adultery.

Normally, when reading the Bible, we need to rely on commentaries and footnotes to understand the ancient Hebrew weights and measures, their farming habits or their currency. No notes, however, are required where sin is concerned. The letter which Paul wrote to Corinth and its Christian community could be posted today to the Christians of Kensington, London, Kensington, New Brunswick, and Kensington, Maryland. We picture the early Christians as saints, breaking bread and singing Alleluias, but Paul was the man on the spot. He writes to the Corinthians in advance, "What I am afraid of is that when I come, I may find you different from what I want you to be . . . and then there will be wrangling, jealousy and tempers roused, intrigues and backbiting and gossip, obstinacies and disorders. I am afraid that on my next visit, my God may make me ashamed on your account and I shall be grieving over all those who sinned before and have still not repented of the impurities, fornications and debauchery they committed."[1]

Men do not change very much. Years ago Ronald Knox, in his *Essays in Satire,* wrote a brilliant essay on the "New Sin."[2] As I recall the story, a learned professor announced that he had discovered a new sin and would disclose it at a public meeting. Needless to say, the Royal Albert Hall was jammed to the doors.

In this final chapter about sin and confession, it may prove helpful to consider the question of change. I find it imperative to face up to change, to distinguish the peripheral from the essential, to become like the householder in the gospel "who brings out of his treasure what is new and what is old."

King Solomon it was who coined the cynical expression "There is nothing new under the sun." To our brave new world with its new deals, new looks, new maths, new morality, new horizons, the preacher in Ecclesiastes has an old and timely message to convey. King Solomon sees us going round in circles like the wind which starts in the south, veers to the north and back again.[3] Or like the raindrops which swell the rivers, are carried out to sea only to go back and begin again, "What was, will be again; what has been done will be done again and there is nothing new under the sun. Take anything of which it may be said, 'Look, this is new.' Already long before our time, it existed. Only no memory remains of earlier times; just as in times to come, next year itself will not be remembered." St.

Paul would gladly endorse this view. It was the constant cult of the new that so disgusted him in ancient Athens. "The one amusement the Athenians and the foreigners living there seem to have," wrote St. Luke later, "apart from discussing the latest ideas is listening to lectures about them."

There is nothing new under the sun, save the various changes of the backcloths against which men play their many parts. We have man on a camel, man on a horse, man in a car, man in a jet, man in a sky-lab, man on the moon. If only we could eliminate men, everything would be new. I still chuckle at an advertisement in an eighteenth-century journal, stating that a certain Señor Jumpedo would, on a certain Sunday, in Vauxhall Gardens, perform the extraordinary feat of jumping down his own throat.

There is nothing new under the sun and yet King Solomon might have wanted to amend his statement had he had the chance of meeting Christ. When you come to think of it, Christ effected a bewildering revolution, the like of which will not be seen again. He gave us everything new, a new covenant, a new birth, to each the chance to slough off the old and to become a new man. His teaching is still new after two thousand years, his sacraments still effective; men still leave home and parents to become his disciples, for his sake men are still ready to lay down their lives. As St. Justin the Martyr put it, "No one has so believed Socrates as to die for the doctrine he taught; no one was ever found undergoing death for faith in the sun."

In an earlier chapter, I introduced Christ as a great psychiatrist. The risk was considerable but worth taking in an age in which so many people depend for balance on their psychotherapist. Christ was much more than a psychologist or faith healer, but this was the side of his character that so many saw first. We watched him drawing to himself many sad, sick, and sinful people, not by bribes or political inducements, but by understanding and sympathy. If he failed with the crowds that wanted to make him king, he was highly successful with a wide variety of individuals, a Pharisee, a prostitute, several fishermen, two tax collectors, a Roman centurion, a permissive Samaritan housewife, and, at the very last moment, a repentant thief.

I called him a psychiatrist, for his approach was personal and inward, penetrating the layers of makeup and impersonation to reach the clown behind the masks. In the isolated world of the heart, where guilt and fear are both endemic, those who met Christ regained a will-to-meaning through his personal love. When Augustine wrote, "Because you loved me, you made me lovable," he touched the deepest point in the human heart.

This, however, is only part of Christ's story, though, sadly enough, I meet many who see no further and who go through life with only half the truth. These are devoted people, drawn to Christ personally, dependent on him as one may be drawn to a doctor, a teacher, a professor with whom one "clicks." With Nicodemus, they go to him alone and after dark. They treasure his words, imitate his every gesture, obey all his precepts so that their left hand does not know what their right hand is doing as they turn the other cheek. Some are mystics, all are Christ-like, but are they Christians in the fullest sense? I suggest that they are covered by the Oxford Dictionary in a secondary definition of a Christian as "one who follows the precepts and example of Christ."

I have to ask myself if this is the whole story and

would Christ have been satisfied with imitation of Christ. Here I am not thinking of Thomas a Kempis' great book, so badly named from the opening words of its first chapter; Professor Allison Peers wanted to see it called "The Book of Friendship with Jesus," very much nearer to the point.[4] The imitation to which I refer is that done in monkey or parrot fashion, the kind of adulation which might have satisfied Bunthorne or Adolf Hitler but never Christ.

In the shortest possible space, for this is no Scripture lesson, I would like to consider in Christ four unusual traits. These, I find, not only help in confession but throw a new light on the imitation of Christ.

(1) Though Christ in his lifetime had power, he had no will-to-power, a point brought out on Good Friday in his dialogue with Pilate and on the previous evening when he washed the apostles' feet. "Tell me, which is the greater, the man who sits at table or the man who serves him? Surely, the man who sits at table; yet I am here among you as your servant." In the training of the first apostles no other subject was raised more often than this.

(2) Christ never used his power to compel anyone to obey him; always the other party had to take the initiative. He seemed to want each friend to act freely and to be himself. Devoted parents and teachers show similar restraint, that the children may develop, not into yes-men, but into men. Hence in the parables which so closely reflect Christ's mind, the emphasis is on initiative and resourcefulness. Even the unjust steward was commended for living by his wits. The two who took the risk and traded with their talents were richly rewarded; as was the merchant who sold all to buy the pearl of great price. Only the timid servant who, for

fear of failure, buried his money in a napkin was severely rebuked.

(3) Though Christ knew all about the heart and the third dimension, he was in practice the complete realist. Though he told us that it is from the overflow of the heart that the mouth speaks, he never saw words as all-important; eventually the heart is revealed as good or bad in the first, physical dimension by the valid test of deeds. "It is not those who say 'Lord, Lord' who will enter the kingdom of heaven but the person who does the will of my father in heaven." One parable, already quoted, puts Christ's teaching in a nutshell; the son who refused to work in the vineyard, then changed his mind and went there, loved his father more.

(4) Understanding human beings as he did, Christ recognized that sorrow and forgiveness must involve the whole man. Sorrow in the heart but not overflowing is as fruitless as a puddle of rain. When Christ dealt with sinners, he catered for all three dimensions, indeed he gave the first clues to that contrition, confession, and satisfaction which Christian tradition later would enshrine. The model confession in the gospel was made by Zacheus. Without being asked, the little publican said, "Here and now, Lord, I give half of what I have to the poor; and if I have wronged anyone in any way, I make restitution of it fourfold." Jesus turned to him and said, "Today salvation has been brought to this house." Poor Judas also acted spontaneously in the first dimension, throwing back the tainted money. He said, "I have sinned in betraying the blood of an innocent man." We have, too, the first trace of a firm purpose of amendment: "And Jesus said to the sinful woman, 'Neither do I condemn thee; go away and do not sin anymore.'"

When facing the winds of change which whistle around my confessional box, I cling to these essentials and let the rest be carried away. If I interpret Christ's mind correctly as he reveals it in the gospel, I must be myself in confession, take the initiative, judge myself entirely on the deeds I have done. All three dimensions want to be involved. Contrition in the heart, confession through mind and tongue, reparation in the physical dimension, these are my concern. The firm purpose of amendment is not as firm as it should be but here Christ promises assistance from outside. The very point of each sacrament is the grace and courage which it was designed to provide. The visible outward sign, made with Christ's authority, gives comfort and assurance to the whole man.

One fact is clear in Christ's lifetime, that the apostles never grasped the meaning of the resurrection or took his words about it seriously. Who can blame them when faced with an occasion unique in history? The excitement of Easter itself and the sudden outpouring of strength on the first Whitsunday compelled them to see Christ and to recall his teaching in a new, three-dimensional way. Thus the breaking of bread, which must have seemed pointless to them on Good Friday evening, now assumed an overwhelming significance. Again, the promise, twice made, that they would forgive sins took on a new and bewildering meaning, when, on Easter Sunday, Christ appeared in their midst. St. John, who was a witness, tells the story simply:

> The disciples were filled with joy when they saw the Lord and he said to them again, "Peace be with you. As the father sent me, I am sending you." After saying this, he breathed on them and said, "Receive the Holy

Spirit. For those whose sins you forgive, they are forgiven; for those whose sins you retain, they are retained."

Earlier in this chapter, I quoted from the dictionary a secondary definition of a Christian as "one who follows the precepts and example of Christ." Such a description may have covered those who knew Christ before he died on Calvary but after Easter Sunday this was no longer adequate. The full definition of Christian becomes, after Pentecost, "one believing in, professing or belonging to the religion of Christ."

Such a definition would have been new even to the apostles until the Holy Spirit opened their inward eye. Now they no longer followed Christ or imitated Christ but they professed and belonged to his religion; they became the founder members of his Church. And at the very center of this Church, as representing the epitome and essence of his earthly mission, were those two great mysteries, the breaking of bread and the forgiveness of sin. Vast mysteries indeed; inconceivable—that is, beyond the range of human imagination; incomprehensible—out of reach of human reason; and yet taught by a simple Galilean to simple people two thousand years ago.

Here we are concerned with one of them, the forgiveness of sin through the sacraments of baptism and penance, the latter known to St. Jerome and others as "the second plank."

The story of this sacrament makes fascinating reading; through it we may watch the mercy of Christ unfolding across the ages and adapting itself to the needs of each succeeding century. History offers reliable guidelines to those buffeted by the winds of change. It sifts the essentials from the nonessentials or, to put it better, the eternal from the transient. If we want to foretell the future, we have only to glance backwards, for there is nothing new under the sun.

Which practices in the ritual of confession may be termed transient? The question of public or private confession might be one. The fashion today is for groups, be they pop, political, or penitential, and this mentality matches the mood of the first Christians in apostolic days. Small, close-knit communities, sharing all in common, the early Christians found public confession and public penance a joy. If our modern penitential services convey Christ's mercy and forgiveness so much the better for us all. What fun we have in store if we return to the ritual described by St. Gregory the Wonderworker, with sinners in grades—mourners, hearers, kneelers, and bystanders—doing their *thing* around the Church.

The early Christian experiment did not last. It fell to pieces in the centuries of persecution when many frightened Christians left the Church. Later these sought forgiveness, and bitterness ensued, comparable to the hatred of collaborators by resistance leaders in Europe after World War Two. Absolution was refused, and un-Christian rigorism was sponsored, chiefly by men who, later, left the Church. The Christian Church rejected such harshness and the secrecy of the confessional was adopted for the penitent's sake. Auricular confession—as it is sometimes called—is thought to have originated in the sixth century, introduced by Irish monks.

The confessional box is transient and there are rumors that soon it will be removed. We take it for granted but, in fact, it is a recent piece of ecclesiastical furniture. St. Charles Borromeo is said to have thought it out and it appeared in the middle of the seventeenth century, fitting the precise, decorous spirit of the

Council of Trent. Further, it afforded scope for elaborate decoration when baroque architecture was at its peak. The confessional box was functional but certainly not essential; we may confess and gain forgiveness anywhere. With a little bit of luck, our last and most significant confession will be in bed. In his *A Priest in Stutthof* the Lithuanian, Father Yla Stasys, describes the practice of confession in a Nazi concentration camp. Polish women, complete with mops and disguised as charladies, sought out the priest in a disused store. "Even though the window already sparkled like crystal," each penitent polished it as she told her tale.

If the confessional box is decorative but unimportant, the same may be said of the various formulas for confessing which men have used. Any number of these which once found favor have now disappeared. Language is forever expanding and changing and the words of an act of contrition which satisfied our grandparents sound ponderous to us today. Whether or not the new rite of confession will prove more apt or more enduring is anyone's guess. The new penitential services annoy some people but give others relief. At best, they attempt in liturgical form to dispose us, to lighten the burden of self-examination which once we had to attempt by ourselves. I see this danger in some of them, that they lessen our sense of individual guilt. By using the word Sin in the singular, not the plural, we escape our personal responsibility. Such a subtle change of grammar is common and intentional in a world obsessed with community. If we say with John the Baptist, "Behold the Lamb of God," it makes a difference whether he takes away the sin or the sins of the world. Dr. Karl Menninger in his *Whatever Became of Sin?* makes the point well: "If a group of people can be made to share the responsibility for what would have been a sin if an individual did it, the load of guilt rapidly lifts from the shoulders of all concerned." There is no true alleviation in such a ploy. The genuine need for personal guilt and personal sorrow safeguarded, new rites and up-to-date liturgies are helpful but peripheral.

One further important item in the ritual of confession seems to me transient. Were it possible to question Christians from each century about the frequency of their confessions, we would need a computer to sift, sort, and catalogue the conflicting replies. Who now knows the habits of sixth-century Celtic monks, of the early desert fathers, of the sturdy pilgrims of the *Canterbury Tales?* It is generally maintained that the first Christians, as adult converts, had small need for confession, their sins were forgiven at baptism. Confession as "the second plank" came later when, after baptism, things went wrong. The frequency or infrequency of confession varies with different people, turns on the three dimensions, is much affected by temperament, environment, even by nationality. The precept of the Church that we should confess at least once a year was not promulgated until A.D. 1215. It applies to those who have committed grave sin, is purely disciplinary, and, according to Suárez, could be altered at any time.[5] That the Church has the authority to make such laws, that much wisdom lies behind them, does not alter their transience.

In deciding the frequency of confession, I have found it helpful to recall the three attitudes to sin. Legally, confession is available at any time, and the Church may legislate that all should go at least once a year. Theologically, the sacrament gives strength as well as pardon and frequent confession proves an abiding joy. Psychologically, we may need advice on the matter but, in the end, we each of us must decide. The present decline in the number of confessions may be a symptom of laxity or it may show a growing maturity in those who were urged to go too often when they were young.

There is nothing new under the sun. I was reared in a devout Catholic home in which confession was infrequent but taken very seriously. Indeed, when, as an earnest young priest, not long ordained, I assisted an old aunt at her death bed, I asked if she would like confession, she answered sweetly, "There is no need, I went last month." At boarding school, frequent confession was first put before us, with no compulsion, merely encouragement. Frequent communion had been introduced and it was thought seemly to confess one's sins in preparation for the Eucharist. So one confessed frequently in term time, rarely in the holidays. As a Jesuit novice, frequent confession became a habit, a sign of piety. I remained a middle-of-the-roader where some colleagues would confess two or three times a week. One settles down peacefully over the years. Now, in the middle sixties, I am back to where I was in early childhood, for the trip to Penzance by helicopter costs too much.

If so much is transient in confession is there anything permanent? To this I would answer with Christ's question at the last supper, "Tell me, which is the greater, the man who sits at table or the man who serves him? Surely the man who sits at table, yet I am here among you as your servant." Poor Peter was embarrassed that Christ should demean himself, and ours should be the same reaction, for these words are not restricted to the last supper but apply in every confessional box. Permanent is the love of Christ and permanent his attitude of service to each sinner; there is no compulsion in the confessional. He wants me to be myself, to take what initiative I like, to engage all three dimensions, to feel the relief of tearing off the mask.

Surely no more curious court of law is known to man. In what other tribunal is the culprit allowed to accuse himself? Even with my devoted parents, I was told what was wrong with me. No police car has ever signaled me to put the question "Would you like to own up to anything?" Only in confession am I defendant and prosecutor; the magistrate is a sinner like myself.

Chesterton in his *Autobiography* put this well:

When people ask me, or indeed anybody else, "Why did you join the Church of Rome?" the first essential answer, if it is partly an elliptical answer, is "to get rid of my sins." For there is no other religious system that does *really* profess to get rid of people's sins. It is confirmed by the logic, which to many seems startling, by which the Church deduced that sin confessed and adequately repented is actually abolished; and that the sinner really does begin again as if he had never sinned . . . the accumulations of time can no longer terrify. He may be grey and gouty; but he is only five minutes old.

G. K. Chesterton's story of his life turns on sin and confession and the recapture of innocence:

I have found only one religion which dared to go down with me into the depths of myself. I know of course that the practice of confession, having been reviled through three or four centuries and through the greater part of my own life, has now been revived in a belated fashion . . . In short, I would not be supposed to be ignorant of the fact that the modern world in various groups is now prepared to provide us with the advantages of Confession. None of these groups, so far as I know, professes to provide the minor advantage of Absolution.

I have often been asked, "What does it feel like to hear confessions as a priest?" Let Newman's lovely passage serve as my reply:

> How many are the souls in distress, anxiety or loneliness whose one need is to find a being to whom they can pour out their feelings, unheard by the world? Tell them out they must; they cannot tell them out to those whom they see every hour. They want to tell them and not to tell them; and they want to tell them out, yet be as if they be not told; they wish to tell them to one who is strong enough to bear them yet not too strong to despise them; they wish to tell them to one who can at once advise and can sympathise with them; they wish to relieve themselves of a load, to gain a solace, to receive an assurance that there is one who thinks of them, and one to whom in thought they can recur, to whom they can betake themselves, if necessary, from time to time, while they are in the world . . . If there is a heavenly idea in the Catholic Church, looking at it simply as an idea, surely, next after the Blessed Sacrament, Confession is such. And such is it ever found in fact—the very act of kneeling, the low and contrite voice, the sign of the cross hanging, so to say, over the head bowed low, and the words of peace and blessing. Oh, what a soothing charm is there, which the world can neither give nor take away.[6]

In the confessional I feel like an unjust steward but one who has cleared it with his master; I ask, "How much do you owe my Lord?" and you say, "A hundred quarters of wheat," to which I answer, "Here is your bill, quick, sit down and write it as fifty."

NOTES

So slight a book should not be asked to carry footnotes, lacks sufficient names to justify an index, and might appear pretentious if saddled with a bibliography. Yet, as a serious work, it should respect the needs of readers who require references. These short notes provide additional information for those who would like to pursue the subjects further for themselves.

1 — Guilty, O Lord

1 Dorothy Sayers wrote feelingly about Christian forgiveness in her *Unpopular Opinions*, p. 14 (Victor Gollancz, London, 1946).

2 Those interested in the penitential practices of primitive peoples should consult *Sin, Its Reality and Nature; a Historical Survey*, edited by Pietro Palazzini and Salvador Canals Navarrete (Scepter Publishers, Dublin, 1964). In the opening article, Giuseppe Graneris writes on the "Concept of Sin in Comparative Religion," with elaborate notes on source books.

3 Dr. Paul Tournier has practiced medicine in Geneva since 1928. Later he acquired psychiatric training and experience "because he learned that many of his patients needed help going deeper than drugs or surgery." Of the two quotations in this chapter, the first is from his *The Meaning of Persons*, p. 115 seq.; the second may be found in *A Doctor's Casebook in the Light of the Bible*, p. 209. (Both books are published in paperback by S.C.M. Press, London.)

4 Professor A. W. Reed describes the writing of Thomas More's *Four Last Things* in his introduction to More's

English Works (Eyre and Spottiswoode, London, 1932). The actual text here quoted is from Rastell's first edition of his uncle's *Works* (1557).

2 — Out of the depths

1 Dr. Viktor Frankl, *The Doctor and the Soul,* Introduction, p. ix (Bantam Books, New York, 1967).

2 St. Teresa of Ávila, *The Interior Castle* (Image Books, Garden City, N.Y.), p. 37; vol. 2 of the *Complete Works of St. Teresa,* p. 207 (Sheed and Ward, London, 1963).

3 Dr. Thomas Harris, *I'm OK—You're OK* (Harper & Row, New York, 1969). The book is described as a practical guide to transactional analysis. It caused quite a stir at the time of publication and has helped many since.

4 Thomas More composed his "Seven Stages of Man" for his own pleasure, when he was still young enough to be living in his father's house. This youthful attempt was first published by Rastell in 1557, a few years before Shakespeare was born. It would be interesting to know if Shakespeare knew of this work and used it. The poet's father was a stanch Catholic and one of his schoolmasters became a Jesuit. The quotation about the actor on the stage, given here, is taken from vol. 1, p. 479 of More's *English Works.* More's description of prayer may be found in his *Life of Picus, Earl of Mirandola,* English Works, vol. 1, pp. 347–48.

5 Archdeacon Grantly's busy morning is described in *The Warden,* p. 116 (Everyman's Library, New York).

6 William James appears frequently on these pages. I quote only from his *The Varieties of Religious Experience,* of which there are two paperback editions, Fontana Books and Mentor Books. Daudet's words may be found on p. 173 (Fontana Books, London).

7 Augustine, *Confessions,* p. 68 (Fontana Books, London), on man laughing alone; p. 167, slightly modernized, on the certainty of free will. Also available in Image Books, Garden City, N.Y.

8 F. Sherwood Taylor; *Two Ways of Life,* p. 35 seq. (Burns, Oates and Washburne, London, 1947).

9 Tournier, *The Meaning of Persons,* p. 159.

3 — Jesus Christ, psychiatrist

1 I trust I am right in omitting the chapter and verse of every gospel text. Such references may easily be traced and I am hoping that sufficient detail is given in the narrative to make each incident clear. Certain key passages affecting this chapter may be listed here. (a) The story of the Pharisee praying in the temple may be found in Luke 18: 9–14. (b) The disciples were told to pray and fast in secret, Matthew 6. (c) St. Peter's great act of sincerity is found in John 21. (d) The good tree bringing forth good fruit is recorded in Luke 6: 43; two verses later we learn that it is from the overflow of the heart that the mouth speaks. (e) The incident caused by the disciples eating without first washing their hands is most fully reported in Mark 7.

2 For the will-to-pleasure, will-to-power, etc. of Dr. Viktor Frankl, *The Doctor and the Soul,* Introduction, p. x. Dr. Frankl, a psychotherapist of international fame, spent several years in a Nazi concentration camp; his first book, *Man's Search for Meaning* (Washington Square Press, New York, and Hodder and Stoughton, London, 1963), in a grim setting, shows what the search for meaning involves.

4 — Thank you, Eve

1 William Golding, *Lord of the Flies,* pp. 154, 223 (Faber and Faber, London). Also available in Capricorn Books, New York.

2   *The Collected Poems of G. K. Chesterton* (11th edition, Methuen & Company, London). I have quoted from "The Pessimist," p. 352; "In Praise of Dust," p. 356; "On Righteous Indignation," p. 184. Also from *Orthodoxy*, ch. 2, *The Maniac*, p. 15 (Image Books, Garden City, N.Y., 1959), and the *Autobiography* (Hutchinson & Co., London, 1937). The final chapter, "The God with the Golden Key," sets out G.K.C.'s views on optimism, pessimism, and confession. I quote from p. 341, and from Maisie Ward, *Gilbert Keith Chesterton* (Sheed and Ward, London), p. 396, for G.K.'s first confession; p. 176 for his views on the fall; p. 546 his plea for Genesis.

5 — Show me the way to go home

1   The three parables here mentioned are set out together in Luke 15.

2   Simone Weil, *Waiting on God*, pp. 166–67 (Fontana Books, London).

3   Salvatore Garofalo provides his detailed study of the prodigal in his article "Sin in the Gospels"; cf. *Sin; Its Reality and Nature* (Scepter Publishers, Dublin, 1964), pp. 63–65.

4   Graham Greene, *A Sort of Life*, Pocket Books, New York, 1973.

5   Thomas More, *A Dialogue of Comfort*, pp. 244–45 (Everyman's Library, New York, 1962). *A Dialogue of Comfort* was written by Thomas More in the Tower of London, awaiting trial and death. It says much for the faith of this remarkable man that this, his last book, penned in a grim situation, contains so many of his best quips and jests. As Professor Chambers put it in his *Thomas More*, p. 299 (Penguin Books, Baltimore), "More's writings in the Tower are more carefree than those which he wrote in freedom; a collection of More's merry tales would draw heavily from the *Dialogue of Comfort*. There is a marked contrast

between the happiness of the *Dialogue* and the grim tone of *The Four Last Things,* written when More was rising to power in the King's service."

6 Augustine, *Confessions,* p. 98, on his first sorrow; p. 197 seq. on his joy.

6 — A lesson from Littlemore

1 Newman, *The Allegiance of Catholics and the Primacy of Conscience; a Reply to Mr. Gladstone,* p. 360, *A Newman Reader* (Image Books, Garden City, N.Y.).

2 Newman, *Development of Christian Doctrine,* p. 365 (Longmans, Green & Co., New York, 1927).

3 Newman, *The Idea of a University,* pp. 203–4 (Image Books, Garden City, N.Y.).

4 Newman, "Sermon on Christianity and Medical Science," *The Idea of a University* (Image Books, Garden City, N.Y.), p. 460.

5 Meriol Trevor, *The Pillar of the Cloud,* pp. 358–59, gives the details of Newman's reception into the Church (Doubleday & Company, Garden City, N.Y., 1962).

7 — The why-therapy

1 William James, *The Varieties of Religious Experience,* p. 443, on confession; p. 95 for the views of Theodore Parker, quoted later.

2 Francis de Sales, *Spiritual Conferences,* p. 347 (Burns, Oates and Washburne, London, 1906).

3 Ignatius of Loyola, *The Testament of Ignatius Loyola,* p. 69 (Sands & Co., London, 1906).

8 — The wind of change

1 2 Cor. 12: 19–21.

2 Ronald Knox, *Essays in Satire,* p. 113 seq. (Sheed and Ward, London, 1928).

3 Ecclesiastes 1: 6–11.

4 E. Allison Peers, *Behind That Wall*, p. 42 (S.C.M. Press, London, 1947).

5 John M. T. Barton, *Penance and Absolution*, pp. 112–15, discusses the decree of the fourth Lateran Council (1215), the comment of the Council of Trent about it, and the precept of the Church about confessing once a year (Faith and Fact Book, Burns, Oates and Washburne, London).

6 I quote Cardinal Newman's passage on confession from *A Newman Anthology*, compiled by William Samuel Lilly, p. 296 (Dennis Dobson, London, 1875). The excerpt is in fact taken by Lilly from Newman's *Present Position of Catholics*.